W9-DGG-640

TO REMEMBER GREGG ANDERSON

TO REMEMBER
Gregg Anderson

Tributes
by Members of

THE COLUMBIAD CLUB
THE ROUNCE AND COFFIN CLUB
THE ROXBURGHE CLUB
THE ZAMORANO CLUB

Printed for private circulation

1949

Prefatory Note

GREGG ANDERSON was killed in action on the Normandy front July 5, 1944. His loss was heartfelt by his many friends, and soon after his death members of the Rounce and Coffin Club of Los Angeles (in which he had been very active) arranged a memorial meeting which was held at the Huntington Library on August 26, 1944.

At the meeting members of the club spoke feeling of Gregg. One dwelt on his personal life, his tolerance, loyalty and uncompromising integrity. Another related incidents in his early association with the Huntington Library. Others recalled him in the print shop and spoke of the varied projects which filled his busy life and his associations with the great of his craft.

In the warmth and enthusiasm of that meeting was born the idea of this book – a project to be shared by those present and by other friends who would join in writing and printing its pages.

The cooperation of other book clubs which had been enriched by Gregg's fellowship was enlisted so that the tribute might be representative of his wide circle of friends throughout the country. He was an early member of the Zamorano Club of Los Angeles and of the Roxburghe Club of San Francisco, and was among the founders of the Columbiad Club of Hartford.

This book of reminiscences, sometimes grave and again lively, reflects the different moods of the Gregg we knew and loved. Here and there may be some bits of typographical history not unworthy of preservation. Gregg might modestly have disclaimed such importance attaching to his activities; he probably would have deprecated the idea of a personal memorial; but he would not have failed to understand the spirit in which his colleagues have recorded for themselves and for posterity their affection for a friend and their high regard for a fellow craftsman.

ROBERT O. SCHAD

Bound by Benjamin B. Kaufman at the Abbey Binders
Los Angeles, California

Contents

§ 1

PREFATORY NOTE *by Robert O. Schad.* Printed by Richard Hoffman at the College Press, Los Angeles, California.

§ 2

MY BROTHER GREGG *by Keith Anderson.* Printed by Grant Dahlstrom at the Castle Press, Pasadena, California.

§ 3

GREGG ANDERSON, THE "GREY BOW PRESS" ERA *by Roland Baughman.* Printed by the University of California Press, Berkeley, California.

§ 4

GREGG ANDERSON IN SAN FRANCISCO *by Oscar Lewis.* Printed by The Grabhorn Press, San Francisco, California.

§ 5

GREGG ANDERSON AT THE MERIDEN GRAVURE COMPANY *by Harold Hugo.* Printed by The Printing-office of the Yale University Press, New Haven, Connecticut.

§ 6

GREGG ANDERSON, HIS YEARS IN LOS ANGELES *by Ward Ritchie.* Printed by Anderson & Ritchie, Los Angeles, California.

§ 7

GREGG ANDERSON—A SECTION OF PHOTOGRAPHS. Printed by The Meriden Gravure Company, Meriden, Connecticut.

§ 8

BIBLIOGRAPHY OF GREGG ANDERSON, 1926-1942. *Compiled by Lawrence Clark Powell.* Printed by the Cole-Holmquist Press, Los Angeles, California.

MY BROTHER GREGG

BY KEITH ANDERSON

MY BROTHER GREGG

TO ME, my brother Gregg was always an extraordinary person. I felt this when we were children; I felt it when we were grown men, and in the many years between. He had a rare kind of wisdom and wit, as well as great kindness not found in many.

Gregg was slightly less than two years older than I. During our childhood, he was always a leader among the boys we played with for he could excel us in all the physical as well as mental activities we took part in. In spite of this, Gregg was something of a puzzle to all the rest—he wasn't quite like them and they couldn't completely understand him. And it was true, he wasn't quite like them, for he had many working qualities about him that are usually reserved for mottoes hanging on walls in boys' clubs, Y. M. C. A.s and the like and not ordinarily found in active operation in small boys. He didn't lie, he didn't cheat, he wasn't petty in the way that most children are at one time or another, and he had a fierce determination about him that was strange to see in one so young.

Most children are given to extravagant talk; they say things just for the saying of them. Not Gregg! When he made a statement, he stuck by it, even though it might have been made at an ill-advised moment and might have worked to his disadvantage later on. I remember a time when we both were being punished for some minor infraction, and the punishment consisted of our being denied bottles of coca cola that had previously been promised us. Gregg, believing that the punishment in no way fitted the crime, a belief peculiarly and solely his own, solemnly averred that from that moment henceforward and until the expiration of one year, he would abstain from coca cola in any and all its forms. He was twelve years old at the time and he liked coca cola, but his word had been given, and his word was not given lightly, so no coca cola passed his lips during that next year. I never knew why he was the way he was in those days; I was puzzled too. As I look back now, it seems that it must have been a combination of two things; an unusual sense of literalness of thought and action that was to be with him always, and the example of kindness, compassion and righteousness set for him by our aunt, Miss Edith R. Sinclair, who brought us up and to whom he was steadfastly devoted throughout his life.

As Gregg grew, his reading habits grew faster apace than his years. At first he read everything he could get his hands on, for he was an enormous reader, but at around the age of thirteen, he became more selective and winnowed out the bad from the good with unerring taste. Our library at home consisted of the usual books found on the bookshelves of the average home. Some were good; some were bad; some were indifferent. At any rate they were many and he knew them all. To the good ones, which he had by this time completely segregated, Gregg affixed his own book-plates and as for the others—well, they should be gotten rid of or kept out of sight.

It was also around this time that he became interested in printing (he printed the book-plates mentioned above). My remembrance of his introduction to printing was that he wanted money to purchase something, quite probably a book, and he could earn it by sweeping out the printing shop of our cousin, Harry Arnold. This he did, and his interest in printing began. That this interest at that time was something slightly less than academic may be demonstrated by an excerpt from a letter I received from him in the summer of 1922 while I was away visiting at an uncle's farm. He wrote, "It sure is fun watching Harry's self-feeder work. A little pair of suckers pick up the paper; two more grab it and lay it on the Tympan; then a thing like a shark reaches down and grabs the paper, pulls it up and lays it on a pile. It sure is a nifty thing; $700 plunks, it ought to be."

From that time on printing was to occupy much of his time and to become his major work. Among other reasons, he liked it, I believe, because it had about it a certain orderliness with such definite lines and borders. He liked orderliness; confusion appalled him. During his high school days most of his spare time was spent in the printing shop, working and printing things that suited his fancy. Perhaps he spent too much time there, for he missed many of the trivial pleasures that boys of that age are accustomed to and probably should indulge in.

Some time after he had graduated from high school, he was offered a job, which he accepted, at the Huntington Library in San Marino. He spent a year there and it was there that his growing interest in fine books and fine printing was immeasurably increased and heightened with each day. He now knew what could be done with printing, what a thing of beauty and good taste it could be.

In spite of this awakened appreciation of printing, he abandoned it almost completely for the next year and a half while he was attending Pomona College. He was too busy, I think, making up for the lost trivialities he had foregone earlier. Gregg enjoyed himself thoroughly while at Pomona and even by his own rigorous standards never regretted what he must have considered time wasted. There were no half way measures with him; when he did a thing, he did it completely, and I'm sure that his entrance into the lighter side of college life was done with the same wholeheartedness that marked all of his past and future endeavors.

After having his fill of college life, Gregg returned to printing by way of the Grabhorn Press in San Francisco. He was to learn much there and also to find out how much more there was to learn about printing. He spent a little over a year there and after a return to Southern California for a short and what he considered unproductive few months he made his way east to seek employment under the guidance of the man he believed the best of printers, D. B. Updike of the Merrymount Press.

While in the east Gregg finally settled in Meriden, Connecticut, and went to work for the Meriden Gravure

Company. He was married there in 1934 to Miss Bertha Hertzman of San Francisco. Their marriage was not to last long, for Bertha, who had contracted tuberculosis, died in 1937 in Southern California where they had returned in a vain attempt to restore her failing health.

Since 1935, the year of his return to Southern California, Gregg had become associated with Ward Ritchie in a printing business in Los Angeles, and their association was continued until his entrance into the Army in 1942. He went into the army with the calm belief that it was entirely the most fitting and proper thing for him to do. His country was at war, and his neighbors and he were equally responsible for the protection of it. He was, I think, the most thoroughly and honestly responsible person I have ever known. While in the Army, he attained the rank of lieutenant. In 1943, while at camp in the vicinity of Los Angeles, he was married to Miss Caroline Bennett of Pasadena.

Early in 1944 his division sailed for England and he was among the many who took part in the now historic and always heroic invasion of the continent. He was always practical minded, a clear thinker who saw things as they were. He never tried to minimize to himself the great dangers that confronted him daily at this time. He was, in his own heart, ready for any eventuality. In one of his later letters to our aunt he wrote, "No one has a right to expect to escape paying a part of the price of winning this war." Well, he paid his price; and I know that it was because of him and the many like him that the war finally was resolved in favor of the Allied Nations.

PRINTED BY

GRANT DAHLSTROM

PASADENA

1949

GREGG ANDERSON

The

"GREY BOW PRESS"

ERA

DESIGNED BY A. R. TOMMASINI
AND PRINTED BY THE UNIVERSITY OF CALIFORNIA PRESS
BERKELEY, CALIFORNIA, U.S.A.

Bread

SONNET BY GREGG ANDERSON, WRITTEN 1928

The silver clash and murmur of the wheat;
The fragile reed that lifts its load and bends
With every shiver that the stray wind sends
Across the field made somnolent with heat,
Until the sun begins his late retreat,
And reapers grateful stop as he descends;
For here's a day well done and hunger lends
A speed to lately weary plodding feet.

Thus rises man and passes as there comes
The scythe of Death to drop him low again.
Who knows what granary this crop will swell?
Or what great maw will gather up the crumbs?
The reaper reaps each day his wheat or men:
His blade is sharp, and naught his mouth will tell.

GREGG ANDERSON

The "Grey Bow Press" Era

IN A LETTER TO D. B. UPDIKE, dated January 1, 1932, Gregg Anderson discussed his introduction to the craft of printing:

> My first acquaintance with it [he wrote] was several years ago, while I was in high-school. I had a part-time job with a printer who had a little shop of his own; he had hired me and set me to work running the press, washing windows, and setting type, so that by the time I had spent three years there, working afternoons and Saturdays, I had a knowledge of the rudiments of the trade. And no more desire to go further than I had to keep going to high-school the rest of my life. I finished high-school and had a chance to work in the Huntington Library. I thought I was happily rid of printing for good. But while I was in the Library I began to see books; books of a kind I had never dreamt of, and for my own amusement I started to print poems that took my fancy and tried to set pages that would please my eye. I read books about Morris and Cobden-Sanderson and discovered "The Fleuron," and began to look for pretty pieces of type display....

It is in regard to that period of Gregg's life that I am now privileged to write, for our friendship, which ended two years ago in Normandy, began during his brief stay on the staff of the Huntington Library. What qualities of mine justified that close friendship I do not know, for we seldom discussed ourselves directly: but for my own part I found in him a gentle, retiring, introspective companion, whose thoughtful approach to every problem was in sharp contrast with my own effervescence, but whose quiet sense of humor was nevertheless deep and genuine.

Above all else Gregg preferred those things which challenged his study and whole-hearted effort. At one time it might have been a complicated title-page; at another the cryptic meaning of a novelist who left most of what he had to say for the reader to figure out; again it was the difficult assignments of college football. But whenever, during the varied chapters of his life, Gregg found that he had reduced a problem to routine or idle pastime, he lost all patience with it, and, if he was forced to continue with it, a violent revolution was presaged. I saw that happen more than once; I know that it happened many times when I was not near to see. That impatience with the commonplace, which I admired in Gregg in 1927, was undiminished when last I talked intimately with him in 1943. Most of us inevitably reflect our traffic with the years; Gregg changed but little, and that little was mainly to let the essentials of his nature shine through more clearly.

IN SPITE of what Gregg wrote to Updike, it is clear that he had decided to become a printer at about the age when most boys dream of driving a locomotive. He was only fourteen when he began working in the printing shop of H. J. Arnold in Lamanda Park, the eastern suburb of Pasadena. Harry Arnold was a family friend—his wife, indeed, was

Gregg's cousin—and he had known Gregg "in and out of his home" since the latter was eleven years old. Gregg liked printing from the start of his acquaintance with it, probably because he always found something new about it to learn; but not a little of his interest is traceable to Harry Arnold's influence.

In fact, Gregg was engrossed with everything connected with books. He thought a great deal about their history and the drama behind their manufacture. Considering his school work, his job, and his friendships, the amount of time he found for serious reading was remarkable, and supplies perhaps the most effective key to an understanding of his nature. There was at that time in Pasadena a second-hand-book dealer, S. F. McLean, in whose shop Gregg was often to be seen reading at the shelves or talking earnestly with the old bookman. McLean was always more concerned with *what* he sold his clients than with the volume of his transactions, and it interested him to find that the boy showed great fondness for the works of George Gissing. Gregg was at that time still in high school, and readers of far greater maturity and much more seasoned tastes in literature usually miss the factors which place Gissing among the Victorian greats.

When, inevitably, Gregg decided to print a book for himself, he chose as the text three critical essays on Gissing by Cornelius Weygandt, Paul Elmer More, and John W. Conliffe. When Harry Arnold asked him how he expected to pay for the paper and binding, Gregg solved the problem in a way that was to become characteristic of him—he examined his finances and decided to print only as many copies as he could afford. The book, which ran to seventy-five pages, sturdily bound in half vellum and blue boards, was issued in only six copies, each numbered at the press. The job was finished in August, 1926, when Gregg had just turned eighteen. The foreword tells the *raison d'etre* of the book better than any other language could:

> My reasons for publishing this book [wrote Gregg] are two: first I wanted to show my appreciation of George Gissing, and second, I wanted to print a book that would be as beautiful as I knew how to make it. I have doubtless erred many times against the canons of fine printing, but I can simply plead my inexperience.
>
> My thanks are due to Harry Arnold who gave me much assistance and allowed me the use of his equipment; also to Miss Edith Sinclair who corrected the proofs.

The Huntington Library had been in San Marino a scant half-dozen years, but the fame of its collections had nevertheless profoundly impressed the youthful Gregg. He did not know that he had made the shoe interchangeable—that the Curator of the great collection, Robert Schad, had also heard of the eighteen-year-old boy who had printed a book by his own effort alone. McLean, knowing that the Library needed promising young men, had mentioned Gregg to Schad, who also was a regular visitor at the bookstore. McLean soon contrived to bring the two men together; they struck up an immediate friendship, and to Schad belongs the credit for giving Gregg his first serious commission, a greeting-card for the season of 1926–27. A few weeks later, after the matter had been discussed with the Librarian, Leslie Bliss, Gregg was invited to come in for an interview, and to bring his Gissing book along. He did so. The possibility of an opening on the staff was broached, and he went away to ponder the proposal and to discuss it with his aunt and guardian, Miss Edith Sinclair, whose home he had shared since the death of his parents many years before.

Not many lads would have gone forward as thoughtfully as Gregg did then. The notion of allying himself with the great institution was not a new one with him—Harry Arnold later said that it had been "uppermost in his mind for some time." Gregg studied the matter for several days, and finally wrote the following letter to Bliss:

After thinking about your offer, I have decided to have you send me the application, if you will be so kind. Everyone I have spoken to has told me that I am foolish to do it; that education is more important; that I shall never go back to school if I stay out, etc. However, I know that I can go back after being out, and also that this would be an experience that I should very much like to have.

About the wages. You told me to name what I wanted for a yearly salary. When I told you what I was getting now, you seemed to think that $1,000 a year might be suitable. You said the work would be odd-jobs, and if that is just manual labor I do not suppose that it is worth more. I do think that I could learn to do anything that calls for a reasonable amount of intelligence, and you can tell what kind of a worker I am after a few weeks trial. I do not want more than I am worth, and I should be happier not to get less than I earn.

And that is my letter. If the application does not contain too many questions such as: "Are you a staunch Episcopalian?" "Is the Constitution of the United States an inspired document?" I should be tremendously pleased to get the job, but I do not change my beliefs for any man's money. I had thought of such a thing as working in the Huntington Library as I had thought of going to Heaven: something to be hoped for but not too seriously considered, and now to have gone even so far as to be writing for an application——!

Gregg wrote that letter on February 12, 1927. Apparently the application form met with his approval, for it was duly filled out, and he was asked to report for duty on the following Monday, February 16.

On that day I met Gregg Anderson for the first time.

We became fast friends at once. Although I was half a dozen years his senior and had worked in the Library since 1924, we were equals in rank—we were, in fact, low men on the staff totem pole. Our work threw us together, and it was work of the most interesting kind. The Huntington rare-book collection was in those days only superficially analyzed, and the turning up of unsuspected treasures was almost a matter of routine. The present classification system was then to a great extent a reality only in the minds of Leslie Bliss and Robert Schad, upon whose excellent memories we depended in our efforts to give adequate book service. For one thing, Mr. Huntington, who died only a few months after Gregg joined the staff, was still purchasing widely. One of the fields in which he was most active was that of modern English and American literature. The staff member who had been concerned with the organization of those books had recently resigned, and Gregg was selected to carry on. In the process of that work he often came across examples of fine printing that had lain unnoticed in the general files, and he fell into the practice of segregating such books for special attention. It was mainly the result of his planning that the Library's file of press books, now numbering thousands of volumes, was organized. Moreover, when he turned up a particularly significant specimen he would show it and discuss it; and thus I too came to learn a little of the criteria of good printing.

He was equally positive when it came to things he didn't like. The fact that a certain book might have a place, due to its content, in the Huntington collection did not impress him if he considered the book to be typographically affected or precious. He loved to segregate little nests of such books and label them with tags that showed his contempt. I recall especially a file of eight or ten volumes published by the "Société des Beaux Arts, Editions de Deux Mondes; limited to twenty copies, of which nine are for America"—on Japan vellum and containing at least three states of each engraving. Gregg put them together and called them "Booby Catchers of the Gay Nineties." There was an even larger number of the folio editions issued by the Paris firm, Goupil & Cie; those he arranged in a single case under the label "Goupil's Gaudy Gap-Fillers." A few traces of his shelf labelling remain even after nearly twenty years. There is a package of currency, for example, wrapped in manila paper on which he had written "$84,000" in at least 96-point figures, and in parentheses just below, in 6-point letters, "confederate."

Meanwhile he still spent much of his spare time in Arnold's shop. He liked to set up sample title-pages—not with any notion of printing the books to which they pertained, but as exercises, and as a means of expressing certain ideas of design which he had conceived. This grew out of his examination of the packets of Laboratory Press projects which were then being deposited in the Library each year. To one of his title-pages (for Hodgson's *The Mystery*) he even proposed to attach a colophon, calling it "Huntington Students Projet No. 1," but after taking a proof and talking it over with Robert Schad, he abandoned that idea. On another he credited me with having translated Barbey D'Aurevilly's *The Last Word,* a work I hadn't known existed.

One morning in April he brought to work a little leaflet which he had printed over the week-end, Ariel's song from *The Tempest,* "Full Fathom Five." The three title words were printed one below another, in progressively deeper shades of blue to symbolize increasing depths of the sea. It was then, I think, that the idea of starting a private press of our own began to germinate in our minds, although it was not for some months that we settled on the name "Grey Bow Press"—"Grey" for Gregg and "Bow" for Baughman. But we did define our purpose, the printing of selected masterpieces in fine format for our own pleasure and for that of our friends—certainly an ideal that had everything but novelty in its favor. We were to use Arnold's equipment as long as he would let us, but we meant to stock some of the newer types as we went along. At the outset my contribution to the partnership was catalytic rather than active;

I knew nothing of printing, and Gregg had more respect for Arnold than to loose a tyro in his shop. Eventually I was permitted to set type, pull proofs, and make corrections, but the day never came when Gregg trusted me to throw type back or to run the press.

In all we issued exactly a dozen items—not counting, of course, the many experimental title-pages or Gregg's other personal ventures. Of the twelve, six were printings of my own verse. Those distant vistas are a little clouded from this proud peak of years where now I stand, and it is no longer easy to see how we could so willingly have wasted so much clean paper and so many tedious hours on my verse. I speak only for myself: knowing Gregg, I am sure that *he* wondered at the time. In fact, his comment to Wilbur Macey Stone, in a letter written in December of 1928, reveals what he would never have said directly to me—"I am sending you something I printed a few months ago. I did it for a friend who hasn't many faults, but who should not write verse."

Most of the early Grey Bow imprints were leaflets, sometimes in wrappers with printed labels, but as often simply folded sheets containing a single poem and a title-page. A couple of dozen impressions usually comprised an edition, and the type was invariably thrown back at once. All of those productions, however, were issued after work had been commenced on our *opus magnum,* "The Quatrains of Curtius," which, though it was long in the making, was really our first project. Soon after the appearance of "Full Fathom Five" Gregg remarked that he would like to do a larger book, something on the order of his Gissing—but what book? I was at once enthusiastic. I had a manuscript. It was poetry, and its personal nature needed to be toned down, but there it was, ready to our hands.

The idea appealed to Gregg, and before the week was out he had issued a prospectus, complete with a specimen of the matchless verse and the proposed title-page, for *One Hundred Quatrains and Twenty Quatrains from the stylus of Curtius Soredd the Elder, now for the first time rendered out of the original Sanswit into English verse by Orvil Baughman.* That we had not yet settled on our press name—that, in fact, we had not even considered the possibility of my sharing in the actual work of printing—is clearly revealed in the prospectus, which specifically divided our responsibilities. I was to be the "translator," and Gregg the printer.

The prospectus promised delivery by July 1, and asked that subscriptions be in by May 15. They actually *were* sent in, to the number of about twenty-five, many of them accompanied by checks. We bought the paper, reached an agreement with D. F. Bogardus, the Library binder, and set to work. Week-ends and holidays were spent in setting, printing, and distributing the type, which we dared not tie up during Harry Arnold's working week. I gave my evenings to revising—usually re-writing—the copy that was to be set up next. Sometimes that revision held up the work for lengthy intervals, and in those intervals other productions were issued. The earliest appeared in July of 1927, an eight-page leaflet containing a song from Arthur O'Shaughnessy's *Music and Moonlight.* It was printed within red rules in the Nash style, and it was the first piece to bear the Grey Bow imprint. Three or four other items followed during the ensuing summer and fall.

Finally, in January of 1928, the "Quatrains" were completed and delivered to the astonished subscribers. Scarcely a statement made in the prospectus remained true. The title-page had been scrapped for an entirely different version, the publication date had been moved back half a year, the quatrains had unaccountably increased in number under the tricky hand of the translator, the price had been raised (except, of course, to subscribers), and the edition had been changed from fifty to seventy-five copies. Belated qualms about the quality of the verse had caused the translator to seek the obscurity of initials on the new title-page.

In after years Gregg and I often laughed at ourselves for the effort that went into the "Quatrains of Curtius"—I, it must be confessed, a little ruefully. Nonetheless, the book served a very real purpose, for Gregg learned much through solving the problems arising from its typographical peculiarities. The project had been much more confining than either of us had anticipated, and after its completion it was only natural that for a time there was a let-down in the activities of the Grey Bow Press. It's hard to be certain after so many years, but apparently something paramount distracted me—perhaps I bought a new car, or fell in love, or even both. At any rate, most of the imprints issued after January of 1928 were wholly Gregg's work, except for one or two poems of mine which I set and he guided through the press.

That year, as it turned out, was not an easy one for Gregg. He was restless and, I think, unhappy. He was concerned about his future and it was clear that he regarded it in very pessimistic terms. He knew that if he was ever to go to college he could not safely put it off much longer. Furthermore, he couldn't make up his mind whether or not he wanted to become a printer. He and Jake Zeitlin talked of forming a really serious private press, but that venture never materialized. One thing was certain—Gregg was becoming less and less satisfied with his prospect at the Library. It was not that his respect for the institution grew less—that never dimmed, and in later years he showed exceptional understanding and sympathy for our particular problems, especially those relating to our specialized publications program. But in 1928 he was going through one of his periodic cycles of dissatisfaction with himself and his surroundings. He hated the very thought of being cast in any mold not of his own choosing. He felt that the Library mold was surely out of his control, and he frankly said to Robert Schad: "As I see it, if I stay long enough and work hard enough I can become a department head—and I do not want to become a department head." A little later, on September 17, he resigned.

Gregg left Pasadena to enter Pomona College at the beginning of the next semester, and we necessarily saw less of each other after that. At first college life attracted him. He made new friends and joined in campus activities, even going out for boxing and freshman football. But again the revolution was not long in coming. After little more than a year at Pomona he once more turned back to the only profession that seemed to have the power to grasp his enduring interest, printing.

This time, however, he took a new tack. With Ward Ritchie (whom he met just before entering Pomona) and Larry Powell he had done a little work at the old Abbey San Encino press in Garvanza; and Arthur M. Ellis, president of the Zamorano Club and a zealous patron of fine printing, had kept a promise of long standing and had obtained a hand-press for Gregg's exclusive use. But Gregg, almost without warning, suddenly decided that he wanted to be a printer, not a private-press man. Dropping everything, early in 1930 he took off for San Francisco in his old Star roadster, to apprentice himself with the Grabhorn brothers. His stay in San Francisco, which lasted less than two years, was a valuable and pleasant experience. He roomed in the home of Hazel Dreis, the noted bookbinder, and became a member of her eager coterie of students and friends. In the group was Bertha Hertzmann, who was later to become Gregg's wife.

In after years Gregg insisted that Ed Grabhorn fired him by resorting to the expedient of temporarily going out of business. Whatever the facts may be, the opening of the year 1932 found Gregg in Boston, with the avowed intention of apprenticing himself with Updike at the Merrymount Press. Updike refused to hire him, but instead gave Gregg something far more rare and precious than employment—his lasting friendship. Both men had the same contradictory qualities, being retiring and positive at the same time, and they developed a mutual respect and affection that is nowhere so clearly revealed as in their frank letters to each other—which each was careful to preserve. From Boston Gregg went on to Connecticut, where for the next three years he supervised the letterpress department of the Meriden Gravure Company. He had found, at last, work that was to his liking.

During all those years, although we corresponded frequently, our friendship slept; there was little to quicken it in the long intervals that separated our meetings. In fact nearly a decade passed before we entered again into the old comradeship. During the summer of 1935 his wife's illness became critical in the eastern climate, and Gregg brought her with him to Pasadena. She died a little more than a year later.

Gregg again joined forces—this time seriously—with Ward Ritchie, whose printing had attracted national notice. Very soon thereafter Ritchie moved his presses out of his living-room into their present quarters on Hyperion Avenue, and Gregg became a partner in the business. At first his duties were largely those of salesman, estimator, production manager, placater of clients, and destroyer of those rats' nests that inevitably materialize in printing plants. From such duties there was little time left for actual work with type and presses, and it was not long before he confided to me that he felt that he was missing the fun of printing. So the Grey Bow Press was revived, and for several years we met each Thursday night at the plant, there to print a few pages (or to discuss the possibility of printing a few pages) of some projected booklet. Our most productive year was 1937, during which three items were issued, with Leon Howard's *The Vision of Joel Barlow* our principal achievement. Later we commenced work on Theodore Hornberger's *Soaring Aloof,* an account of the first balloon ascension in America, but that work never went beyond the proving of the first section. Many others joined in the venture—Dave and Suey Davies, Ted Hornberger, Carey Bliss, Dave Palmer, to name only a few. The project languished when we became preoccupied with the Rounce & Coffin Club's "Western Books" exhibitions. Then the war broke out. When he left for O.C.S. Gregg placed in my care the copy and proof-sheets of *Soaring Aloof.*

I cannot close this account of my friendship with Gregg Anderson without recalling the long walks in the San Gabriel Mountains we used to take together on Sundays after his return from Connecticut. Most of the trails on the Pasadena slope have known our footsteps. On two occasions we went farther afield—two occasions that stand among my most cherished memories of Gregg. In the summer of 1939 we spent ten days in the high country back of Yosemite Valley, working our way from camp to camp. The next year found us again in the Sierra, this time with our tent pitched on the shore of rainy Bullfrog Lake, just over Kearsarge Pass at the ten-thousand-foot level.

Those outings mark the high point of our friendship, and they had perhaps a deeper significance than I realized. Not before or since were we ever so close. The diverse facets of Gregg's nature were more clearly revealed on those occasions than was possible in our casual, work-a-day meetings. On the one hand were his reactions to the sombre realities of his life—the still-fresh tragedy of his first wife's death; the stern pressure he was under in building a successful printing business during the trying later years of the depression; his growing conviction that his chosen profession needed to be rid of the parasitic "fine-printing" influence, to make way for more honest and essential standards.

On the other hand I had glimpses of a side of his character that was being developed gradually but surely—an increasing capacity for enthusiasm, animation, and, most of all, for happiness. All of us who knew Gregg then were convinced that he stood on the threshold of distinction. His objectives were sharp, clean, and tempered by experience; in his profession he was accepted as one whose early promise was being richly fulfilled; as a man he was looked up to for his sincerity, his standards, and his utter dependability. In a sentence, his life was unfolding, and he was becoming the figure everyone had instinctively felt he would become from the time he was a lad in his teens. The word "happy" is not one to be loosely applied to Gregg—on one occasion he asserted that he couldn't even define the word. "People think they are happy," he said, "when in fact they are only exuberant, or contented, or even merely free from discomfort or insecurity." Nevertheless, when last I talked with him in the summer of 1943 it was plain that he had at last a confidence in himself and a zest for his future that few men ever realize, and for which most men would gladly trade their chance of "happiness." He was eagerly looking forward to his coming marriage and to the life which could not be planned but which surely lay ahead in the unopened years. As he once said to Caroline Bennett, the girl who became his wife so few short months before his division sailed for Europe, "I have spent my first thirty-five years preparing for my thirty-sixth."

WRITING THIS brief account has not been easy. Our relationship was strong, but it was intermittent over some fifteen years. In consequence, whenever I think of Gregg—as I do more often than I realize—it is to recall some particular thing he said or did on some particular occasion. As, for example, the almost unique instance when I saw his temper overcome, for a moment, his natural reserve. We were walking away from Arnold's shop one Saturday afternoon in 1928. He had been silent for a long time. Suddenly he took a quarter from his pocket, looked at it sourly for a second, then drew back his arm and threw the coin as far as he could. "What good is a quarter when that's all you have?" he asked bitterly, more of himself than of me.

Or the time in Yosemite when he left me to my fishing, which he disliked. That night he showed me how he had spent his afternoon. He had written a couple of rattlesnake stories—"because," he explained, "I'm tired of hearing the same ones over and over." It was true that although the faces that reflected the light of the main camp-fires each evening might be completely unfamiliar, the principal topic of conversation was invariably rattlesnakes, and, as invariably, all of the anecdotes so carefully certified by personal experience had been told by others the night before, also with full personal certification. Gregg gave me his compositions, "The Affair of the Four Rattlesnakes" and "The Affair of the Five Rattlesnakes." We planned to fill out the cycle from one to ten for publication by the Grey Bow Press, but they remain today in their original form.

There were literally clouds of mosquitoes around us as we walked down through Vogelsang Meadows, where patches of summer snow remained to furnish them with good breeding-places but little food. They were young and vigorous and eager for their very first meal. As I fought them off I watched Gregg extend his bared arm, hold it still for a moment, then slap it sharply. "It's no use trying to kill them one at a time," he said. "Besides, according to the laws of natural selection I should be able to create a tradition among them that it is fatal to bite Gregg Anderson." His "Quarterbook" condensation of *The Origin of Species* had just been published.

About 1938 we began a project that was designed to make our reputations. We were enthusiastic admirers of the printing bibliography by Bigmore and Wyman, and we decided to see what could be done about bringing it up to date. For months we collected entries from dealers' catalogues and other lists, mounting them on cards for filing. I don't know how many we made or where they are now.

Once as we climbed a high pass in the Sierra Gregg followed me up the steep trail with short, chugging steps. I had gotten far ahead, but when I stopped to catch my breath he passed me and went on to the summit. He later explained that he had decided that shuffling steps require less horse-power than long ones, and are therefore less tiring. Neither logic nor rhetoric availed me, for he insisted that scientific experiment is more reliable than theory. And he had the final word. On one of his army leaves he told me that soldiers are trained to climb mountains according to his method.

Though days and weeks sometimes go by without my thinking directly of Gregg, subconsciously I still expect that any moment he will walk through the door with a set of proof-sheets or a new proposal for our after-hours effort. Others who were close to him have told me that they know that feeling too. But even when some definite action, like the chance turning over of a book that he had given me or that we had printed together, or the writing of this inadequate memoir, brings his memory sharply into focus and reminds me of the reality of his loss—even in such moments it is the reality that is the impossible.

THIS ACCOUNT opened with an excerpt from Gregg's first letter to Berkeley Updike—the man he came to admire perhaps above all others—and it can be fittingly closed with one from his last letter to that venerable and scholarly printer, written on December 15, 1941, just two weeks before Updike's death:

We had our first black-out last week. It lasted about 2½ hours. The radio was the chief means of relaying the news. "By order of the Federal Communications Commission and at the request of the Fourth Interceptor Command a complete light black-out is called for, effective immediately." That was repeated over and over for fifteen minutes, until it was drummed into your soul. We heard the sirens going, but they were very faint. Finally the radio went off the air, all street lights out, and we sat in the dark until it was over. I don't think anyone was prepared for it—much less for the war. I feel as if we were all on a giant roller-coaster at the top of the first long downward plunge. We can see what is ahead—we begin to realize what we have to go through, but we can't feel it, we can't really understand it. Just as well, no doubt.

ROLAND BAUGHMAN

Gregg Anderson

IN SAN FRANCISCO

GREGG arrived in San Francisco some time in 1931. He had an old Maxwell car and he had driven up from the south on the chance he might land a job at the Grabhorn Press. He hadn't bothered to tell anyone he was coming. If the Grabhorns happened to have a place for him, fine. If not, he would at any rate see the shop that had produced some books he admired. Good printing was already an obsession with him; it remained an obsession as long as he lived.

Ed Grabhorn had a couple of large jobs on hand, and Gregg knew how to set type. He went to work. Within a week he was a fixture about the place; he remained about two years and everyone was sorry to see him go. He had a mild manner and a slow, reserved smile. He was then about twenty-two, or perhaps a year or two less than that, which made him the youngest member of the staff. The staff itself was small and, as always, unpredictable. The reason for this last must be that the place naturally attracted nonconformers: the over-solemn or the earnestly literal-minded gave it a wide berth. There were eight regulars during most of Gregg's stay: Ed and Bob Grabhorn, Jack Gannon, Bill Bissell, Valenti Angelo, Tom Hewitt, Old Man Adams—and Gregg. Ed and Bob presided respectively over the press and composing rooms. Val had his drawing-board beside the window of one of the front rooms, overlooking Pine Street. Adjoining it was the composing room where Bob, Gregg and old man Adams held forth. Ed and Tom operated the presses in the rear, and Jack was general utility man.

During that period I had a loose and informal connection with the shop and spent an hour or two there late afternoons, answering such letters as got answered, sending out bills, supplying copy for the announcements of new books, and sometimes — if the current publication looked thinner than it ought to look—writing an introduction that would pad it out to a respectable bulk.

Saturday mornings Ed would stop by long enough to sign a couple of sheets of blank checks and I would come over about eleven-thirty and make out payroll checks. When they were ready Jack or Gregg or Val would take them down to the bank and cash them and we would all go to lunch.

It was at one of these Saturday lunches that someone—it was probably Jack Gannon—proposed organizing the Pamphlet Club. The rules were simple. Each member was required to write and set up a pamphlet — and to print only enough copies to supply the other members. On the day a member completed and delivered his pamphlet he was automatically expelled from membership. Gregg was intrigued. The idea appealed to his lively sense of the appropriate. The trouble with most clubs, he maintained, was that they aimed at self-perpetuation; here was one that sensibly provided for its own dissolution the minute its usefulness ended. The last time I saw Gregg — in 1941 — he still held that opinion. "Too bad we didn't go through with it," he commented. "We really had something there."

"Leaves of Grass" was being printed — two folio pages at a time — when Gregg arrived and first he worked on that. Later he spent many weeks setting up "Red Badge of Courage" — a very long book to be composed by hand. He had a consuming interest in every phase of the design and printing of that work, and for a while he considered doing a treatise (in pamphlet form) that would trace the book's evolution from the first trial pages to the finished product. With this in mind he gathered up every proof that showed any change in the typographical scheme. Within a month his collection numbered more than two hundred specimens. Thereupon Gregg gave up the idea as impracticable and sadly consigned his proofs to the ash-can.

Bob and I had meantime embarked on a publishing venture—the Westgate Press—and the shop printed our books during times when it was not busy with more pressing jobs. Whenever we were ready to announce a new Westgate title the members of the Pamphlet Club were invited to an evening mailing party. Gregg and Jack and Val always showed up, and usually George Harding, who had once studied printing under Updike at Cambridge. (It must have been because of George's enthusiasm for Updike that Gregg, when he left San Francisco, headed for Boston.) On mailing nights the Westgate Press magnanimously paid for dinner for the crowd. It is pleasant to recall too that the group shared in the one and only division of Westgate profits. Sometime in 1932 – the year before prohibition ended–it was discovered that the firm's liquid assets had reached a point where it seemed both safe and desirable to declare a five-gallon dividend. Someone hurried to the telephone and called Tony.

That summer Bob took a trip back to Indianapolis, his home town, and one Saturday at lunch the Pamphlet Club voted to send greetings to the absent member. The group returned to the shop and spent the afternoon setting up broadsides. Gregg's was patterned after the posters early California sheriffs used to post on barn doors offering rewards for the capture of road agents and other reprehensible characters. It's too bad this broadside has disappeared; today it would be a prime item of Greggandersoniana.

When he reached San Francisco Gregg knew exactly what he wanted. His ambition was to learn the printing trade from the ground up. Following the ancient custom, he apprenticed himself to a series of skilled craftsmen; meantime he studied the theory and history and traditions of the craft, for he was ever the student. He already knew the rudiments of printing when he came up from the south; during his stay in San Francisco and Boston and Meriden he perfected himself, working under the ablest teachers he could find. By the time he had completed the circuit and returned to Los Angeles his apprentice days were over. His work during the remaining years of peace shows how well he had learned.

After he joined up with Ward Ritchie and their shop became Anderson & Ritchie, Gregg was busy, but not so busy but that he occasionally got up to the bay for a few days. He was then the West Coast agent for the Meriden Gravure Company and his San Francisco visits were thinly disguised as sales trips. But Gregg never let matters of business interfere overmuch with these brief vacations. He would come into the office, prop his portfolio of samples against his chair, and spend an hour or two reminiscing about the Grabhorn-Westgate days; sometimes we would call George Harding and the three of us would continue the discussion at lunch. In those days Harding and I frequented Sam's, a lunchroom in a nearby alley, which we firmly—and correctly—believed served the best coffee in town. It was a mere hole in the wall, but if Gregg ever had misgivings about the place he kept them to himself. Only once did he venture an indirect comment on our taste in restaurants. One noon while we were perched on our stools against the wall the telephone began to ring. Sam was too busy to answer and the ringing continued for some time. At last Gregg leaned forward and said: "Sam ought to answer that. Somebody wants to reserve a table."

Gregg's San Francisco friends heard from him occasionally after he entered the army, first from a camp in Arkansas, then from Georgia where he was undergoing the rigors of officers' training. After that he was clearly too busy to write, and the next word we had was the appalling news from Normandy.

In sorrow and regret the Pamphlet Club symbolically hung out a gold star.

—OSCAR LEWIS

PRINTED AT

THE GRABHORN PRESS

SAN FRANCISCO

1949

GREGG ANDERSON

AT THE

MERIDEN GRAVURE COMPANY

MERIDEN CONNECTICUT

1946

GREGG ANDERSON
AT THE MERIDEN GRAVURE COMPANY
1932–1935

GREGG ANDERSON came to work at the Meriden Gravure Company in Meriden, Connecticut, on March 7, 1932. Paul Johnston was foreman of our letterpress department and we had in process a book to be published by the Huntington Press of New York titled "Man Makes His Own Mask" by Bob Davis. It was a collection of Davis portrait photographs with biographical paragraphs about each man. The type had been set in galley form in twelve-point *Poliphilus* on the Monotype and we were planning to re-stick it when making up the pages and needed a good compositor.

Gregg was suggested to us as a possible employee by Richard Ellis who at that time was operating his Georgian Press in Westport, Connecticut Ellis had heard of Gregg's availability through D. B. Updike of the Merrymount Press in Boston. Gregg had left the west coast early in the year with the idea of coming east to try to get a job at the Merrymount Press. Nineteen hundred and thirty-two being a low spot in the depression there wasn't enough work at Merrymount, or in fact in most any printing plant in the east, to make getting a job very easy. However, Mr. Updike apparently took an extreme liking to Gregg and, which was unusual for him, made considerable effort to find a place for Gregg. When he arrived in Meriden to go to work, he was flat broke. He had even to walk from the railroad station to the plant because he didn't have bus fare. How he managed to get along until he got paid, I don't know, but he never let on the fix he was in nor asked for any advance.

Gregg took hold immediately and it was obvious that we had secured an exceptional workman in him. Not very many months after he came here Paul Johnston left to go to Woodstock, New York, and it just seemed natural to put Gregg in charge of the department. It was just a short time before he had things running pretty smoothly in a department that at Meriden Gravure we had always regarded more or less as a necessary evil. Generally speaking, the only letterpress work done in the plant was in printing plate numbers and legends.

Gregg stayed pretty much to himself during the first few months he was in Meriden. He didn't get acquainted with many of the other employees, and we discovered that he was spending a lot of his evening hours in the plant working on jobs and, as was typical of him, he neglected to punch the time clock. When Parker Allen, president of the company, discovered this he put Gregg on salary with an increase to compensate somewhat for the considerable amount of extra work he was doing.

One day Gregg told us some of the things that he had been in the habit of doing on the Pacific

Coast—little booklets, jobs that he had done for himself while working for the Grabhorns, and also when in Los Angeles with Roland Baughman of the Huntington Library. He asked for permission to use the plant equipment to do similar things on his own time.

Gradually, I began to get better acquainted with Gregg. At that time my closest friend in Meriden was Kenneth Thornton, assistant advertising manager of the Manning & Bowman Company. We used to spend two or three evenings a week together, mostly frequenting the neighboring speak-easies. I asked Gregg if he wouldn't like to go out with us occasionally. After becoming better acquainted with us Gregg suggested that we were wasting a lot of time and possibly we might want to find something more sensible to do, which was just his way of calling our attention to the wonders of printing. He agreed to teach us as much as possible of what he knew and we met at the Meriden Gravure Company a couple of nights a week for two or three hours and then stopped at our favorite "speak" on the way home. It wasn't long before Ken Thornton tired of the evening work and dropped out, but Gregg certainly sold me on the interests one could find in printing, and finally felt that I had progressed far enough so that we could do a small book together. We decided to reprint *Some Early Notes on Early Connecticut Printing* by Albert Carlos Bates, librarian of the Connecticut Historical

Society, a paper which was originally printed in the Papers of the Bibliographical Society of America. The composition of this was my test as a compositor and, if I remember correctly, I set every line. Gregg, of course, designed it. We did about seventy copies on odds and ends of scrap paper. I don't believe there were more than ten that were printed on any one particular kind of paper. The little booklet was bound in boards by the J. F. Tapley Company of Long Island City through our friend Bob Wessmann, president of that company.

As soon as that was finished, and the seventy copies had been distributed to friends and to printers we wished to have as friends, we started looking around for something else to do. As I remember, we had several discussions over Tom Collins' at Tom Conheady's speak-easy in Wallingford, and finally Gregg agreed to write some notes on recollections of the days he spent at the Grabhorn Press. We both worked on the book, but there is a lot more of Gregg in it than there is of me. The little book was well received. When Ward Ritchie and Jake Zeitlin heard of our plans, they wanted a few copies for the Primavera Press. Finally Gregg agreed that we would print up thirty copies with that imprint, and the figure charged for those thirty copies covered the cost of binding the edition which numbered seventy copies. The book was finally published in 1935, shortly before Gregg left Connecticut to return to the Pacific Coast.

One day in May 1934, Gregg announced to me that he was leaving next weekend for New York to meet his bride-to-be. Until that time I don't believe anyone in Meriden knew that Gregg as much as looked at a girl, but it developed that he had been corresponding daily with Bertha Hertzman who had been left in California when Gregg came east with the idea of working at the Merrymount Press. The plant was pretty busy at the time and Gregg and Bertha's honeymoon amounted to Memorial Day weekend which was a day longer than the usual weekend. Gregg had rented a furnished apartment on Lincoln Street, Meriden, and they had a very nice little home there.

It wasn't long after Bertha came to live in Meriden that she became ill with tuberculosis. Apparently it was a recurrence of a condition she had had before coming east, and the New England weather did not agree with her too well. She finally had to be moved to Gaylord Sanatorium and was there for some considerable time. Gregg visited her two or three evenings a week and Saturday and Sunday. Many a Saturday afternoon I drove down with him to see Bertha.

It was a downhill pull for Bertha and it wasn't too long before she had to be moved to a sanatorium in West Haven, Connecticut, a place where they had facilities for handling patients in advanced stages. Finally the doctors suggested that the best thing for her would be to try to get her back to

Southern California. They left New Haven on July 6th, 1935.

At the time Gregg left, we had plans made for the third publication of our little private venture, and by that time had also secured a name for the press—The Timothy Press—the name Timothy coming from the second, fourth and fifth official printers of the State of Connecticut, Timothy Green. The title of the book was *DeVinne & Marion Presses*, a chapter from the autobiography of Frank E. Hopkins. Gregg completed the design of this in Los Angeles and the actual production was carried on in Meriden. The book carried the imprint of the Columbiad Club and was published early in 1937.

This brings us to the beginning of the Columbiad Club of Connecticut. I went to the west coast in the fall of 1934 as I had for two or three years previously, and came back much impressed with the accomplishments of the California book clubs, The Book Club of California, the Roxborough of San Francisco, the Zamorano, and Rounce & Coffin of Los Angeles. Gregg and I got to talking over the possibility of establishing something similar in Connecticut. In December 1934 we decided to do something about it. One Saturday afternoon, we drove over to Windham, Connecticut to visit Ned Thompson. We had heard of him and knew his work, but had never met him. We spent a most delightful afternoon at Hawthorne House. Ned was enthusiastic about forming a printers book club. We then journeyed down to New Haven one afternoon to call on Carl Rollins of the Yale University Press. The idea met with his enthusiastic approval as it was something he had had in mind for a long time. Parker Allen, president of the Meriden Gravure Company, was whole-hearted in his support, and finally in January 1935 we were able to call a meeting to discuss the possibility of forming the organization. Because the men present at the first meeting and a few who joined immediately after were close friends of Gregg, I list them herewith: Parker Allen, president of the Meriden Gravure Company, Meriden, Connecticut; Valenti Angelo, who at that time was living in Bronxville, New York, having moved a short time before from San Francisco and his work at the Grabhorn Press; George T. Bailey, then manager of the Yale University Press; Jack Davis of the Case, Lockwood and Brainard Company of Hartford, Connecticut; Quincy Emery, paper merchant of New York and resident of Old Greenwich, Connecticut; Carl Rollins, printer to Yale University; Ned Thompson, proprietor of Hawthorne House, Windham, Connecticut; Paul Alcorn, librarian of the Connecticut State College at Storrs, now University of Connecticut; Crompton Johnson, rare book seller of Hartford, Connecticut. These last two were not at the organization meeting but were both present at a meeting shortly thereafter and were men that Gregg had a chance to know well before he left again for the west. At the first meeting,

Gregg and I brought along the remaining copies of *Recollections of the Grabhorn Press* as a gift to those present at the organization of the Club. The enthusiastic reception of this gift was the main reason for starting the Columbiad Club "Keepsake" series and at the next meeting of the Club Quincy Emery supplied Keepsake No. 1 which was a map of Connecticut printers cut in wood by Charles Smith. Gregg, all during his period in Meriden, was in touch with Mr. Updike through occasional visits and correspondence, and when Gregg wrote D. B. Updike of the plans of the Columbiad Club. Mr. Updike sent along photogravure proofs of Baskerville's portrait that was used in Josiah Benton's Essay which he printed for the Club of Odd Volumes. This became listed as Keepsake No. 2 to members of the Club. Gregg was one of the sparkplugs of the group and while he was only with us a short time his interest in the Columbiad Club didn't wane even after he had returned to Los Angeles. When his Keepsake was due he could be depended on to be ready on time.

I'm not quite certain, but I believe Gregg is responsible for the name "Columbiad Club." It seemed to be extremely difficult to find an appropriate name for the group, and it was finally decided to take the name of Joel Barlowe's *Columbiad* which was probably the first attempt at fine printing done in this country by Fry & Kammerer at Philadelphia in 1807.

During the years that Gregg was in Meriden, we became close friends and when he had to leave I felt very badly and I believe he felt somewhat the same. We had an opportunity to continue our close friendship, however, because my work brought me to the Pacific Coast usually in the fall of the year, and I had opportunities to visit with him in the fall of '36, '37, '39, and '40. Gregg's contact with the Meriden Gravure Company continued, as he handled our Pacific Coast business from the time he arrived there and was still officially listed on the Company rolls "on leave of absence for duty with the armed forces" at the time of his death.

HAROLD HUGO

C P R

THE PRINTING-OFFICE OF THE

YALE UNIVERSITY PRESS

THREE HUNDRED FIFTY COPIES PRINTED

[FIFTY IN PAPER COVERS]

Gregg Anderson

HIS YEARS
IN
LOS ANGELES

I MET GREGG ANDERSON IN 1928. It was through W. O. Waters of the Huntington Library, who had long been a friend of my family. I had recently become interested in printing as a career, but inasmuch as I knew nothing whatsoever about the trade, I went over to the Huntington Library to get their advice on how to make a beginning. Mr. Waters told me about Gregg, who had been working at the Library for a year and a half but had left that fall to go to Pomona College as a freshman. He arranged that we should meet one week end when Gregg would be home in Pasadena.

Gregg couldn't have been over 19 or 20 at the time but he seemed very mature. He was over six feet tall, quite thin, with a sallow complexion. His hands you always noticed—his fingers were very long and graceful.

While he wasn't exactly the athletic type, he tried out for freshman football at Pomona. He remained a substitute until the last game—the big game with Occidental College. Midsemester examination then thinned the ranks of those eligible, and Gregg graduated to the first team. There may be a record of the outcome and score of that game but Gregg never mentioned it. And that was for all practical purposes the end of his indulgence in athletics. He hiked and fished with Roland Baughman, and may have played some sets of tennis or bowled five or six times in later years, when dragged away at lunchtime by the men in the shop, but that was all.

His early taste in literature and typography was advanced for his years. He started out when he was fifteen, printing a book about George Gissing. Poe, Yeats, Housman, Ralph Hodgson, D. H. Lawrence, Llewelyn Powys, and A. E. Coppard were favorites of his in his teens. At Pomona he went in for the "moderns" of the twenties. Typical was an announcement he printed in 1929. It was *moderne* without any capitals:

two whippersnappers believe that everything that is good is green, but that desirable things are not good. for this reason they are throwing away their books and want you to pick some up. besides they have seven water colors by laudermilk that remind one of lemon satin dreams. there are drawings by the wife of the laudermilk, there is an etching, and there are stray copies of blast, new masses, transition, new adelphi, hound and horn, ed howe's monthly. the place to find all this is 347 west sixth street, claremont. you may not discover it on your first attempt, but it's there, right behind number 341. this shop has practically no hours. you may have to break in. but that is agreeable to the proprietors.

The other young whippersnapper was John Cage, Gregg's roommate, who has since become known as a composer and director of ultra-modern music.

Bruce Rogers, Francis Meynell, and Porter Garnett were then Gregg's idols in printing. He was attracted chiefly by their versatility and their happy use of printer's ornaments. With Roland Baughman during 1927 and 1928, under the imprint of the Grey Bow Press, Gregg experimented to his heart's content. He enjoyed arranging title pages out of type and ornaments, and printing fragile pamphlets of a single poem. He liked original arrangements and thus may have taken a lot of liberties with his ornamentation and type. He was not altogether satisfied, however, and sent out examples to people he thought might give him constructive criticism. Porter Garnett was one of these. He was director of the Laboratory Press at the Carnegie Institute of Technology and was pressed for time by his duties. However, he wrote Gregg several long and detailed letters of criticism, from which I quote a typical excerpt, dated April 29, 1928:

You say, "I did not know it was wrong to use italic numbers and brackets." I wouldn't put it that way. There is no rule against using them. Don't think in terms of rules. Rules are for people who cannot think for themselves, who are not intelligent, I tell my students. "Learn how to break rules—wisely." There are, however, principles—principles of taste. Do anything that looks well (rule or no rule), that adds grace, charm, beauty, dignity to your work. Don't, on the other hand, do a thing, produce an effect, which destroys or detracts from grace, charm, beauty, dignity. That is an aesthetic *principle*, not a rule. You add, "I can see that they (italic numbers and brackets) are rather weak and wishywashy." In using them you did not break a rule, but violated a principle. You introduced something that detracts from the seemliness of your page. You *see* it when your attention is drawn to it, but you should *feel* it beforehand.

I don't now remember whether Gregg and I met first at his house or mine, but I believe it was at mine in South Pasadena. It was in the latter part of 1928, either November or December. I had just enrolled at Frank Wiggins Trade School in Los Angeles to learn the rudiments of typesetting. Gregg took a great deal of interest in my plans, and within a few days of our first meeting he sent me a parcel together with the following letter:

I am sending you some stuff of which I have duplicate copies and a few things which I printed. The letters from Porter

Garnett will give you an idea as to where I fell down, and they also give you an idea as to what kind of a man he is.

I hope that you can read the list of addresses that I send. You will be able to get some fairly good-looking things from some of them, and for nothing.

I used to send samples of things I had printed as an excuse to write a letter to some, and they generally answered in a quite amiable fashion.

The list he sent consisted of about 25 names and addresses of fine presses issuing prospectuses and catalogues, and of booksellers selling finely printed books. In addition, he sent me his copy of the *Fleuron #5*, Frederic Warde's *Bibliography of Bruce Rogers*, and Porter Garnett's *Laboratory Press*.

It was also in 1928 that Gregg was elected a member of the Zamorano Club. He was by far the youngest person ever to be elected to that Los Angeles book club. Arthur Ellis, who at that time was president of the club, had an abiding interest in printing. In his back yard he had housed a Colt's Armory press and some type with which he used to print occasional things. He became interested in Gregg's printing and when Gregg left the Huntington Library to start at Pomona, he proposed to buy an Albion hand press and install it at the college for Gregg's use. The press was ordered from the Caslon Company in England, but during the eight or ten months before it could be delivered, Gregg became involved in so many other things that he temporarily lost his interest in printing. He wrote me in June 1929, "I have given up most of my plans regarding printing."

Arthur Ellis' hand press had arrived a month or so before this, but Gregg had "run out on him," as he wrote. At the same time he said, "Probably you have the use of all the type that you want, or I would offer you mine. It will just be lying around in odd corners gathering dust for some time."

I had finished my apprenticeship at Frank Wiggins Trade School and was working at Vroman's Book Store in Pasadena together with Lawrence Clark Powell. After Gregg's letter, Powell and I made arrangements with Clyde Browne, who had a printing shop in a strange, romantic edifice known as the Abbey of San Encino. It was near the Arroyo Seco in Garvanza, a suburb of Los Angeles. Besides the printing shop there was a chapel, cloisters, a dungeon, and several studios up on the hillside. We rented one of these studios with the added privilege of using the presses on evenings or Sundays.

All the type I had was some 14-point Garamond, so I took advantage of Gregg's offer and invited him to join Larry and myself in our off-hour project at San Encino. He had spent his summer vacation from college working on a ranch in the San Joaquin valley. By the time September came around he once more felt he'd like to do a little printing. "Think of it, reduced to the point where I haven't even a letterhead," he wrote in accepting our offer. He further suggested our getting Mr. Ellis to allow us to use the Albion press, but by that time Grant Dahlstrom and Jake Zeitlin had put it together in Arthur Ellis' garage and, as the "Ampersand Press," were producing their first books on it.

We didn't actually get organized for much printing until Christmas vacation. Gregg had long wanted to do a book to give to the Zamorano Club. In fact, he had started it a year or so before, had printed a few pages which he hadn't liked, and had quit. With our new setup operating, he revived this project, "Body's Breviary," by Joseph Warren Beach. It was a piece which he had read in the *American Mercury* and had liked. He got permission to print it from the publisher but never heard from the author until after it was printed. Hence, his colophon read: "Of an edition privately pirated by Gregg Anderson, this is copy number—."

From the standpoint of design this was the first mature piece Gregg had done. It was restrained, delicately designed, and well conceived. He was once more interested in printing and tired of college. Just as thoroughly as he had entered into the activities at Pomona a year and a half before, he now dropped them. If any of the classes in which he was enrolled bored him, he quit attending. He had passed his twenty-first birthday and had received a small inheritance. He bought a secondhand car and books—mostly books printed at the Grabhorn Press. He wanted to become a printer again and, as Grabhorn was his new idol, it was not strange that when the semester was over he got in his car, came by Los Angeles to say good-bye, and headed for San Francisco to see if he couldn't get a job with the Grabhorns. He did.

His letters of that period start out quietly enough. In March 1930 he writes:

I like my job up here quite well. All I have done so far is distribute and set type for the Whitman, and from the looks of things, that's what I'll be doing for the next couple of months, as there are still 200 pages to print. Nice place, San Francisco; I guess I'll be able to stand it for some time.

By the end of April he had moved into the huge house on Franklin Street where Hazel Dries had her bookbindery and where half a dozen young artists, printers, and bookbinders had rooms. He had printed himself a letterhead and was making plans:

I may start printing something pretty soon. A fellow living here wants to illustrate a book, so we may do *The Song of Honour* by Ralph Hodgson. . . . You should see the fine oil painting I got today. Valenti Angelo gave it to me. I had him make me a bookplate to give to Francis Stock and he threw the painting in to boot. A good painting, too.

Gregg, always shy with new people, was beginning to make friends—and here with this truly Bohemian group, probably for the only period in his life, he had a completely unrestrained, uninhibited, hilarious time.

Life at the Grabhorn Press was always interesting. Gregg wrote a small book in 1935, *Recollections of the Grabhorn Press*. Earlier he had pictured the shop to me in a letter:

The books Ed finds are something fantastic. He never spends less than $300 a week for books, and that is only the obvious purchases, the books he brags about, or the ones he orders by mail. He shows up at noon waving a book that he has just bought, the *Flowers of Passion*, George Moore's first, an immaculate copy that he just unearthed down the peninsula 90 miles or so. Or a dandy early map of California, his latest, that is to say, during the last two years—bent. California, Californiana, anything, everything, books by the truckload, magazines, letters, newspapers, land grants, early oil paintings, engravings of the great fire of 1850, manuscripts of Overland journeys.

He supports six or seven book peddlers who appear daily at the shop with a book that they will let him have for $10 and which he buys for $2.50. When he is away for a week or so they become noticeably thinner. A hunted look appears. He returns. The joyful welcome. The Zellerbach collector comes prowling. "Well, I'll have some money at the end of the week." He staves them all off with additional work and $100 on account. "To hell with them, the robbers, that last bill was too high anyhow, and I just gave them a check six months ago."

And Valenti. "God, but the ad business is awful. No work. My neck, my belly, my back, I won't live a year longer. My wife, my baby, my painting. You bastards, you don't know what art is. You haven't any emotions. I can feel that's the way. The Red Badge ought to be illustrated. I'll be somebody when you're still puttin' those little things in a stick. I'll go to New York. I'll go up and live in the mountains, raise some apples and have a few pigs and play with the baby. The world's coming to an end. A fellow stopped me on the street and I gave him a quarter yesterday. I've got to stop buying books. I'll sell every one I've got. You wait. I tell you we're in for a hell of a time. Money's scarce. The world's comin' to an end. Oh, my back, my belly (I can't eat this stuff, I know, I worked at the St. Francis), my side aches."

And Tom. He runs press. "Thackeray makes my ass ache. Where was I last week? Oh, I was down at the library doin' a little research. Yeh, I'm gettin' old. Almost sixty. I had a good job in New York. Running a string of platens. Worked for a Jew and he was a hell of a good boss too. Best job I ever had. De Vinne? All he had was a bunch of old junk. Why, I wouldn't touch it. I was used to handling good machinery. Say, this woman has a damn clever style. Say Bob, ain't this supposed to be Juniper instead of Junior, and there's a couple a bum letters here too. Give me a brass lead and I'll jimmy the form. Drunk, sure I'm drunk."

In time, Gregg began to revise his sights under the influence of George Harding (an ardent admirer of D. B. Updike) and Bill McDonald (who had come to the Grabhorn Press from John Henry Nash. He wrote toward the end of June 1931:

Just what do you think of fine printing by now? The last six months have seen me gradually losing my awe and reverence for most of it. I have been reading De Vinne and I have become a De Vinne fan; there was a man who knew more about the making of books than all the modern practitioners thrown together. Scholarship, learning, intelligence, those are the things that now seem to me the ingredients of a good book: more than all the art in the world they are the essentials. I find Ed's utter disregard for the logical arrangement and correctness of the text getting on my nerves now and again; his inability to make a book that can be read standing in the way of my appreciation of his other good and true qualifications as a book-printer, so I busy myself at learning how to spell, tracing growth of the foot-note in an effort to imbibe a learning that will make me competent to print McKerrow's next opus—have you read *An Introduction to Bibliography*—or a book of poetry.

Gregg once told me that Ed Grabhorn could never bear firing anyone even when things were in the doldrums, as they were toward the end of 1931. Instead he'd just announce that he was through and was going to close up shop. Everyone would be paid off and away they'd go. A few days later Ed would be at work again and gradually the indispensables would drift back and the pared-down staff would work on what books there were to do.

In November 1931 Grabhorn closed down and Gregg came south to Los Angeles. During the time he had been in San Francisco I had left Vroman's Bookstore and had gone to Paris and worked for Francois-Louis Schmied. I returned to Los Angeles in the early fall of 1931 and after working a month at Jake Zeitlin's Bookshop fell in with some fellows I'd known at college who had recently started a printing shop. It consisted of one Chandler & Price press and a few cases of type in the back end of a store. The front end was well taken up with a reception room and three nice offices for Messrs. Hackett, Newell, & Ritchie. We had an old pressman who couldn't set type, but that didn't matter much because the bulk of our work was forms for the local Presbyterian Church, of which one of our firm was a member, and for a local insurance agent, a cousin of the other member. By the time Gregg arrived on the scene, we had dug up a couple of commissions for small books to be printed, so Gregg was hired as compositor and lockup man. The setup lasted only a few months before all the invested funds had run out and there was no way to continue paying the staff. We had printed, however, *Libros Californianos* by Phil Townsend Hanna and *The Songster* by Mona Kenaston, together with a catalogue for Dawson's Book Shop, and two interesting booklets, *Stars Do Not Make a Noise* by James Stephens and *In Galilee* by Hildegarde Flanner.

Gregg went up north for a visit and I wrote him about a new plan—a colony of artists and artisans out near Riverside. If we wished we could be the printers in the group. He sent me a note:

I'll drop in at the shop some time Thursday and we can talk some more about Riverside. I don't know anyone I would rather work with than you, but it would mean doing something that does not quite jibe with my present ideas, and besides that, giving up another plan that I have had for some time.

I learned, when we met on that Thursday, that, no longer believing in "fine printing" as such, the Riverside deal smacked too much of the art colony for him. Also, he maintained that he didn't know enough about printing yet to be on his own and wanted a few more years' experience in large shops. And finally, he mentioned that he had already written to Daniel Berkeley Updike and hoped to get a job at the Merrymount Press.

The refusal from Mr. Updike was caustic enough to have deterred anyone but Gregg. He, however, was determined to go east, and nothing could stop him. He left around the first of February 1932.

On the 28th of February Gregg wrote from Boston:

I have been waiting patiently for something to happen so that a letter would be of some value, but with the usual laxness nothing goes on happening from day to day.

So you can see that while Mr. Updike has been good and kind, he has not allowed himself to be brow-beaten, and I look about for other brows to belabor. Believe no slurs about the man for he is worth quite a trip if only to talk to; and I have talked to him, been taken to his club for lunch, to his home for tea, and spent an evening with him as well.

He is a little, tiny, dried-up sort of a fellow, a good deal like a needle. A very clever talker, witty and charming, and full of stories, and by no means tied up in his printing. Not sentimental, but not altogether lacking in sentiment. I had expected something much more caustic, and found that he is quite urbane; expected him to be brusque, and he goes out of his way to give me directions here and there, tells me what I should see, gives me a card to the Atheneum, and letters to all the printers he knows. I think he feels a little responsible for me, as if he had lured me out of the west and here I am, and what can he do about it.

But he still does not feel that he is bound to hire me. I am sure I do not know the technique of breaking down his resistance; maybe there is none. However, he set me right on one point. Writing personal letters to him without being introduced first is an A-1 crime. That was no kind of a letter to write. So when I had the opportunity to write to the Meriden Gravure Company which had responded slightly to a line I wrote them, I took it around to him before mailing it, and he pruned and clipped it into what he thought was a business-like and straightforward form, and then off it went.

But he tells me that when he hires someone, he wants someone he can boss, no bright young fellows with suggestions to offer. And he doesn't want someone with ambitions, who will work a while and then off for the woods. He might hire me, he said, if he needed someone to set type, but no quicker than he would anyone else who came along. And he has all the typesetters he needs at present, thank you. So I have given up hope, as far as he is concerned.

I have seen Pottinger, been to the Riverside Press, and visited various other printers and publishers without much success. And I have written letters that produced nothing, aside from the one I mentioned. And so the two weeks have passed.

As to my trip here, it was quite alluring. I landed in New Orleans in time for the wind-up of the Mardi Gras, and had a day there to parade the streets and keep my eyes open. Just like a big circus, but a damned nuisance as far as getting a room was concerned. I spent hours going from hotel to hotel, and finally landed in a place ostensibly a hotel, but I have my doubts about the morals of some of the lady roomers. However, I had just spent four nights sleeping catch-as-catch-can, so I didn't go looking for trouble.

Spent part of a day in New York without any desire stirring in me for more, and here I am, safely ensconsed on Beacon Hill, for a time at least. Beacon Hill is an absolute phenomenon in America—the old residential district in the town about five or six blocks square of three- and four-story homes. Imagine a complete street of buildings without a single one that is offensive. I am delighted with it. One gets the impression that here is a culture, or here are the remnants of a culture, and the only one in the country, no matter how the smart boys whip it around a stump.

He got the job at the Meriden Gravure Company. Paul Johnston was the foreman of the composing room, and Gregg worked under him. At first he was supposed to help with the fine printing, but soon he found himself spending more time on the General Electric and International Silver Company jobs, to which, apparently, no one had paid much attention.

He wrote:

I'm really a lot more interested now in correctness than how a thing looks. I tell you, sometime you should sit down and read De Vinne's four books through, and I will bet money you can't look at printing with the same eyes again. The man knew so much, he had such good sense, that he opens your eyes to the superficialities and trivialities of a lot of the present laborers in the vineyard. His taste may not have been impeccable, but he makes up for that in other ways.

I feel much more satisfied about printing and my future as a printer than I ever did before. I could never feel sure that some day I was going to be able to set pages like Grabhorn or Bruce Rogers; I felt pretty sure I would never be able to, because it was nothing that could be learned; you could or you couldn't, that was all.

Now I have decided that I don't care. I have discovered that there is another way of printing that I can learn—it will take years, I know, but to be able to start off in any direction is much better than simply wandering around in circles looking for the unknown. So much for my state of mind.

When Paul Johnston left Meriden in June, Gregg took over his work and, soon after that, the job of the proof-reader too. So he had a busy summer, even though election year doldrums had hit New England.

He wrote on August 28th:

It is a peculiar thing, but this job of mine which I was so loath to take and so anxious to get out of, is turning out to be the best thing I ever got into. They made me foreman of the type room last week.

A year later he brings in a new note:

May take a fling at a little private printing again. Harold Hugo, one of the boys in the office, wanted to learn printing so we've been practicing after hours, and have finally started on a booklet, *Early Printing in Connecticut.*

Although Gregg had become an important part of the Meriden setup, and was happy there, in 1935 he began thinking of returning to California. A year or so earlier he had married Bertha Hertzmann, a young bookbindress he had met while living at Hazel Dries' in San Francisco. She was unwell in the east and the doctors thought she might do better in a more reasonable climate. So that July they moved west to Pasadena.

Gregg and I talked over the possibility of his joining The Ward Ritchie Press, but at that time there didn't seem to be enough of an opening. Earl Myers was running the presses, and I was doing whatever else was necessary. These were still depression times when a printer was lucky to eat, and we were barely managing that.

For a month or two Gregg floundered around. He worked awhile for Bruce McAllister in the composing room of Young & McAllister. Then he worked out an arrangement for himself as typographic advisor for the Huntington Library. In this capacity we saw a lot of him. He suggested that he could bring in work to us on a commission basis, and soon was out trying it—with a certain amount of success. When he brought in a job, he would take off his coat, put on his apron, set the type, pull a proof, and be off to the customers with it in the green Model A Ford roadster he had bought when he first returned to Southern California.

Rather soon it developed there was enough work coming in to keep Gregg busy, along with the rest of us, without his going out to get his own jobs, and he went on the regular payroll. Soon afterward, Joe Simon joined the organization and began setting type for us.

The Ward Ritchie Press in 1935 was not the practical De Vinne kind of an establishment Gregg had glorified in his letters. Started in 1932, it had outgrown its original home—a barn in South Pasadena and, since the summer of 1933, had been located in an old hillside ranch house in Los Angeles. The house itself had been built long before there was any thought of the city's encroachment, when all of the surrounding hills were grazing land for cattle. A stream had flowed down in the valley and a small mill had been built on the other side of it, almost directly across from our place. These buildings were the only two landmarks left of the pastoral days. The stream had been piped underground and its bed covered over. Two broad and busy concrete highways sped along the bottom of the valley. The hills were covered with a thousand houses clinging in tiers, as in a Riviera village.

This progress had left the old ranch house isolated from one of the boulevards by a high-cut bank, but there was still an ample plot of ground and it was well surrounded by a grove of fifty or sixty eucalyptus trees. Before we moved the shop there, it had been necessary to dig a curving driveway fifty feet up through the bank and brick it in. This was done and a great deal of other work by the time Gregg became associated with us.

The shop was shaped like an L, with a string of five studio windows reaching from floor to ceiling all across one side, giving quantities of light. In the toe of the L was the press room with our two presses, a Galley Universal and a Colt's Armory; in the heel was our Washington hand press, which we used as a proof press; and up the sides of the leg ran our type cabinets. A brick fireplace furnished warmth when it was cold, and a grandfather clock pounded out the time. We had had a grand piano in one corner, often having music with our work, but this had been removed to make more room.

In the back of this and up a few steps was a stockroom, with a paper cutter and ample space for storage. The library-office was off to one side of the main room. It was also up a few steps and had a separate entrance to the outside. Around the walls, ceiling high, were our "books about books" and examples of printing—two or three thousand of them.

The walls of all of the rooms were of pine planks, which we had whitewashed, and on them were hung book pages, type specimens, and engravings. It was a very pleasant place to work and to visit—so much so there was an almost continuous stream of visitors, both day and night.

That phrasemaker, now U.C.L.A.'s librarian, Lawrence Powell, was one of the most constant loiterers. He nicknamed the establishment "Ritchie's Road House," at which suggestion Gordon Newell, the sculptor, cut a large tavern signboard which was hung from a post at the foot of the steps down by the street. It portrayed the anchor and bull's head, which we had adopted as a mark from Antonio Espinosa's first new-world printer's mark. In 1934 Paul Landacre had engraved in wood the first version of it which we had used on the title page of one of the two books we had in the "Fifty Books" that year. By the time Gregg joined us we had a half dozen variations, good and bad.

Gregg never criticized this happy-go-lucky, rather haphazard printing establishment we were then running, but through the years he gradually maneuvered us toward a more practical, businesslike establishment. From the very first he spent many overtime hours in the shop, and usually some time on Sunday, cleaning out cases, sorting leads and slugs, wrapping paper scrap, or distributing type. He had a mania for order. His whole life was orderly. On weekdays Gregg always arrived immaculately dressed in a suit. He would hang up his coat and put his metal line gauge in his back pocket. This was his badge, whenever he was in the shop. Then he would start work. When noontime came he would take a book and his lunch, which he always brought from home, and go outside to sit on the steps in the sun. Even his lunch seemed to follow an invariable pattern. At least to my recollection it never seemed to change during the years, always ending with a Hershey bar.

The books he read during his lunch hour were reserved for that time alone. He would never carry one of them home to finish at night. There he had other books. Each noon he would pick up at the sentence where he had left off the day before and continue for the half hour he devoted to his lunch. I remember the first book he picked out for his lunch hour reading in 1935. It was Tymperley's *Encyclopedia of Printing*—over a thousand pages set in double columns in a small eight-point type. Gregg started on page one and after a year of noon hours he completed it. Undoubtedly he is the only person who has ever accomplished the task since Tymperley himself read the proof in 1839. After Tymperley he took on the many-volumed Gibbon's *Rise and Fall of the Roman Empire*. Earlier in his life, he once told me, he began with Volume I and read through all five feet of the Harvard Classics, with hardly a pause for breath. He was an omnivorous reader and the number of serious books he went through was staggering. He wrote a few months after he had arrived in Meriden and just after Paul Johnston had moved away to Woodstock:

> Since I can't go visiting the Johnstons any more it turns out that I'll traipse around a little. I tried passing time since they left by a sort of endurance reading contest and had to give that up before going blind. I'd sit down Saturday afternoon and read straight through till Sunday night. Disposed of several books I wanted to read, but I decided it wouldn't do. And before Paul left I had pretty well read through his collection of books on printing, *Manual of Typefounding* by Fournier, Dard Hunter on paper-making, *John Bell* by Stanley Morrison, *Bulmer and Bensley* by H. V. Marrot, a book on William Pickering, *John Baskerville* by Ralph Straus, etc. Oh, I was going great guns. Later with just the public library to draw on, I flashed through *Diana of the Crossways* by Meredith, *Origin of Species* (say, that's good), *Data of Ethics* by Herbert Spencer, Shaw's *Intelligent Woman's Guide to Socialism and Capitalism.* But there are too many books in the world; I can't read them all.

On Sundays, with us, Gregg relaxed somewhat. Both his appearance and manner were casual in comparison with what they were on weekdays. Instead of an immaculately pressed suit, he wore a leather jacket and spent his time wandering around the place, puttering, cleaning up, and making plans for the future.

We made plenty of plans during the seven years we worked together, and many changes took place in our Press. A few months after he had started working with me he announced one day that he had five hundred dollars which he had saved and that he would like to become a partner. With his investment we made a down payment on a Miehle Vertical, and that was the beginning of the firm which eventually became "Anderson & Ritchie: The Ward Ritchie Press." For four years I had been using the name of The Ward Ritchie Press after having first considered San Pasqual, Adobe Flores, Bella Union (all from local history), Flame, and Shandy. I tried out most of these names on early books but my indecision was such that John Slocum, for whom I printed a small book on the hand press in the summer of 1932, would have none of my alternatives, arguing that I would change my mind before the next book was printed. He was the one who insisted on The Ward Ritchie Press, and it became the easiest solution for a name.

In 1940, with customary candor, Gregg announced that he would like to have his name in the firm. Heretofore, we had never troubled to have a formal partnership agreement, but with a new name to consider we went all the way and made the firm a legal identity. After discussing the matter with numerous friends, we decided it would be silly to drop wholly the name, The Ward Ritchie Press, so we decided to retain it for what publishing we might do and use Anderson & Ritchie for our commercial printing. For the legal name we combined the two, cumbersome as it is.

The acquisition of the Miehle Vertical press increased

our production to the point where we soon felt the need for more space. We had Ted Criley design us an addition to our existing building, but the city of Los Angeles stepped in and rezoned our property from business to residential income, and we were forced to search for a new location. I had recently received a small inheritance and we were able to put a down payment on a bleak and lonely two-story building on poetic Hyperion Avenue, halfway between Lyric and Fountain avenues. We moved our equipment there and commenced business on a new, larger, and more professional basis in January, 1937.

Gregg gradually managed to make our operation a businesslike one. We acquired first of all a professional proofreader, of which there have since been several fine ones—J. C. Taylor, Cecil G. Smith, Forrest Ganger, and Dow Parkes. We also acquired a full-time secretary and an accountant, and we put in a cost system. Immediately he joined me, Gregg insisted we could never succeed without a cost system. Our previous practice had been to throw in an extra color, and an illustration or so, if the book we were printing pleased us enough, though this raised the devil with profits. One day Gregg noticed an ad in the *Pacific Printer* by a San Francisco accounting firm for printers. It was headed by J. C. Gilkerson. We wrote him a letter, liked his reply, and hired him to reorganize our system.

In 1931 when Gregg and I were working at Hackett, Newell, & Ritchie, at the suggestion of Arthur Ellis, we helped organize a book printing club, whose beginnings are best described by Lawrence Clark Powell in the little book *Ten Years (Almost) of Rounce & Coffin-ism.*

The origins of the Rounce & Coffin Club are already shrouded in mystery. Only one fact is irrefutable: it was founded by an itinerant book-peddler and a band of starveling printers—Jake

Zeitlin, abetted by Gregg Anderson, Grant Dahlstrom, and Ward Ritchie—back in the bitter autumn of 1931. Thus it would seem to have been the product of social unrest and unemployment. Or, in other words, the materialized figment of disordered young brains, all of them hungry for business. For Satan finds some mischief. . . .

The first meeting was held at Jake Zeitlin's home in the hills of Echo Park on November 19th, 1931. Since I was the least busy at the time, I printed the announcement, using the name of the Thistle Club in honor of Bruce Rogers. This meeting set the pattern for the subsequent years of the club's history—controversy, heckling, good fellowship, printing, and wine. After much argument, and upon the suggestion of Jake Zeitlin, the combination of those parts of the handpress, Rounce & Coffin, was substituted for Thistle Club. It is a name that mystifies the curious layman even unto this day. The club's existence was lusty but intermittent during the years 1931-1935, while Gregg was in the East. The occasional meetings were rotated at the homes of members, whose number had been considerably augmented since the first session. But the schedule of time, place, and subject was haphazard until Gregg's return from Meriden. Thereupon the Rounce & Coffin meetings became a regular monthly ritual.

Gregg began the revival by getting his old friend, Roland Baughman, and myself to meet as a planning committee. We had dinner several times at a restaurant on Lake Avenue, near Gregg's home in Pasadena. I have forgotten whether it was by election or by our arbitrary selection (though I suspect the latter) that Baughman was made permanent secretary of the club. At any rate, between him and Gregg the activity of Rounce and Coffin was revived and its monthly programs planned. The Constance Hotel in Pasadena, with its convenient bar, was made the headquarters for our dinners. Previously, announcements of meetings were made with an elaborately printed notice, but Gregg eliminated this folderol and substituted a simple card which he produced each month on the platen press in our shop. Their appearance never varied during the years he made them, which was until he left for the Army.

Also, Gregg was responsible, to a great extent, for the Exhibition of Western Books, patterned somewhat after the Fifty Books of the Year Show of the American Institute of Graphic Arts. In 1938 the Rounce and Coffin Club decided that they would try to stimulate interest in fine printing as produced in the Pacific Coast states. Several members of the club gathered at our shop on evenings during the fall of 1938 and helped print announcements and entry blanks for the first show. It was quite a success, and thirty-five books were selected from the many which were submitted by western printers. Grant Dahlstrom, then at Adcraft, printed the first catalogue. Subsequent catalogues were printed by the University of California Press, Stanford University Press, the College Press of the Los Angeles City College, and our own press, but all of the preliminary announcements and forms for the years until 1942 were planned and printed in our shop by Gregg. Because of the war and his departure, the project was dropped in 1942, to be revived in 1946. In its way, the Western Book Show is a memorial to Gregg Anderson's devotion to printing and his persistence in fostering it.

Another extracurricular printing activity in which he was interested at this time was the revived Grey Bow Press. Gregg and Roly Baughman began coming to our shop on Thursday evenings to set type and print some small things for their pleasure. Soon they were joined by Dave

Davies, his brother Suey, Dave Palmer, and Ted Hornberger. More good fellowship than good printing resulted, but there were a few small projects finished, of which the *Noel Barlow* was the most important.

During the seven years Gregg worked with me he seemed more interested in the production than in the design of the books we printed. He worked out the format of the books and catalogues we did for the Huntington Library, and a few others, but he seemed to prefer to have me make the layouts, leaving the responsibility of the proofreading, the makeup, and the presswork to him. As a result, I had the front office and most of the contacts with the authors and he had his desk back in the shop, midway between the composing and press rooms. In back of his desk he rigged up an arrangement of cubbyholes, one for every person on our staff. Whenever he made a suggestion to any of us he would also make a note of it and stick it in the proper box. Periodically he would check on us.

He also took responsibility for the appearance of the shop, and as a result it was always as clean and orderly as his meticulous nature could desire it. Neatly printed notices were hung prominently around the place: "Keep the shop clean," "Check to see that the form is properly backed up," "Flush the toilet," "Turn off power on leaving," etc.

In 1935 Gregg began playing with the idea of a series of condensations of great nonfiction books, to be sold at twenty-five cents. The first title selected was Darwin's *The Origin of Species*, and Raul Rodriguez made the condensation. It was issued under the general name of *Quarter Books* in a yellow, red, and black format about the size of the *Reader's Digest*. Gregg's blurb read: "Here is a book that everyone should read. Most of us have picked it up at some time or other, and then put it down . . . because the type was too small . . . or because it looked too dull and dry. Now *Quarter Books* brings it to you in a new format designed for easy reading; with a clear legible type, short lines, and carefully edited and condensed to give you only the important points of the book. This is a book you can talk about for weeks; think about for months."

Future publications announced on the inside back cover were: *Progress and Poverty* by Henry George; *A Greek Anthology*; *A Roman Anthology*; Boswell's *Johnson*; and a series of outlines of astronomy, geology, mathematics, etc.

This adventure started out bravely with an experimental printing of 1,000 copies, but we were never able to develop a method of distribution for them, though we tried the American News Company and all other means we could think of. Except for the printing, it was pretty much Gregg's personal venture, and he must have written two or three hundred letters in his attempt to get the book sales moving. Whether he was just a little too early in the field of inexpensive paper-bound books, or whether this title was too forbidding, is a question. Anyway, hardly anyone bought *Quarter Books* except the University of California bookshop in Berkeley. Slowly, over a period of years, they exhausted the edition and seemed genuinely disappointed that we were not only allowing the first title to go out of print but that we had not produced the others we had announced.

In addition to commercial printing, from 1932 until Gregg joined us in 1935, The Ward Ritchie Press had printed about forty-five books. From the time of his arrival until he left for the Army in the fall of 1942, we completed something over 100 more. In 1937 Joseph Lica moved in on us with his Linotype machine, and a year or so later Ben Kaufman joined us and began gathering equipment for binding our books. With the addition of Cas Duchow, an artist, it became possible for us to do all of the work connected with the making of books, except for engravings, right in our own shop.

And that was the favorable condition of things with us in December 1941, when the Japs attacked Pearl Harbor.

Today it is hard to realize how bleak the outlook was on the west coast during the first year of the war. Most of our own printing business was with libraries, colleges, and institutions, or with collectors and persons who wished to have books privately printed. Almost immediately after the declaration of war, most of our customers concluded that printing was one of their dispensable activities. For six months we tried to keep our organization intact, though we hadn't enough business to keep the men going even one or two days a week. By mid-June the situation was so bad that Gregg and I concluded that the shop could not support both of us and that one of us would have to get another job. Since I had a family and he had none (his wife, Bertha, had died not long after he had returned to California), we decided that I should get another job to tide us over and allow us to keep our organization together.

Within a few months Suey Davies, Paul Monroe, and Angelo Tortarola were taken into the service and it seemed probable that Gregg would also be drafted. He attempted unsuccessfully to enlist in several selected branches. I remember him "boning up" on aircraft terminology for a glider pilot examination. He was turned down but in November 1942 was drafted and sent to Camp Robinson in Arkansas for his basic training. Gregg could always look on a situation objectively, and he was intrigued by the effectiveness of Army methods of teaching. After a few weeks he passed his test for a marksman with a score of 155 out of

200, just nine points below a sharpshooter. Since he had never had a gun in his hands before, he credited this achievement to the careful preliminary training the Army was giving. He liked the food. He enjoyed the training and was impressed by the overall efficiency of the Army.

After his basic training he took a three-week pre-officer training course and was then sent on to Fort Benning, Georgia, from which he graduated as a second lieutenant in the infantry. After further moves to Camp Roberts, California, and to Camp Barkeley, Texas, he was assigned to Company B, 359th Infantry, of the 90th Division, and trained during the fall of 1943 in the desert around Indio, California.

Gregg was not one to complain of hardship, and in a letter to Charles Adams in which he gives a graphic picture of the conditions under which they lived during maneuvers—long marches, C Rations for breakfast and dinner, little or no sleep (and some of that in slit trenches), freezing nights, only half a canteen of water a day—he writes:

> But sometimes we can sit down and look at the sky, and the sun is good and warm in the daytime, and there is no rain on us, and no bullets—and we decide it could be a whole lot worse.

In October, between maneuvers, Gregg was married to Caroline Bennett, a Pasadena girl he had known for a long while. He had filled out physically and was bronzed and strengthened by his hard year in the Army. When he left us in California for the last time, around the first of the year, he looked healthier and happier than I had ever seen him. He spent two months at Fort Dix, New Jersey. Part of the time his wife was with him and together they were able to visit the many good friends he had made while working at Meriden.

In March, 1944, his division sailed for England. It was spring when he arrived and he found it "incredibly beautiful to one who had never seen anything like it before—the hedgerows coming into leaf and the trees into bloom; the fields dotted with sheep and lambs."

His division landed in Normandy on D Day and he fought through with them as far as Pretot. For his bravery on July 3, 1944, he was recommended for the Bronze Star and made a first lieutenant. His posthumous citation reads:

By direction of the President (and General Order 28, Section III, 1944, of the 90th Division) the Bronze Star Medal was awarded by the War Department on 8 March 1945 to First Lieutenant Gregg S. Anderson for bravery in action in ———. On 3 July 1944 as his company was advancing, two men on the right flank were wounded by enemy fire. Lieutenant Anderson crawled 25 yards under increasing machine gun fire to give them first aid, then made two trips through this hazardous fire to bring the men to safety.

Two days later, July 5th, he was killed in action while leading an advance patrol.

In addition to his talents as a printer, Gregg had great ability in writing. His letters were as fine and interesting as any I have ever read. The few things of Gregg's which were published show his keen sense of humor, his insight and discernment, together with a felicitous use of language.

In 1929, while a freshman in college, he won first prize in the Jennings English Contest for excellence in the use of written and spoken English. This amounted to several hundred dollars. Also, while attending Pomona, he was a member of the Scribblers Society. However, it was not until 1934 or 1935, when Harold Hugo prevailed upon him to write his *Recollections of the Grabhorn Press*, that the delightful quality of Gregg's prose was really discovered.

This book is a minor classic and only the fact that but seventy copies were printed has kept this from being more widely recognized.

The balance of Gregg's writings was of a scholarly or critical nature. In 1938 the production managers' magazine, *PM*, prepared an article on the Merrymount Press. Mr. Updike, however, would have none of it, and suggested that they have Gregg write one instead. His analysis and appraisal of the books of the Merrymount Press appeared in the issue of October-November 1938.

In Volume III, Number 2, of *Print*, published in the summer of 1942, appears a like appraisal of the books of the Grabhorn Press. This was originally prepared as a talk for the Rounce & Coffin and Zamorano clubs, as was *The Dictionary Page*, which was published in *Print*, Volume 4, Number 1, Winter 1946-46.

In 1941, when the Henry E. Huntington Library was planning an exhibition of the work of the Merrymount Press, they requested Gregg to help in planning it. Mr. Updike died during the preparation and it became a memorial exhibition. Gregg arranged the exhibit and wrote and designed the catalogue. He admired Daniel Berkeley Updike more than any person he had ever known, and this last literary work of Gregg Anderson's was a fitting tribute to the man he wished most to emulate and whom he eventually might have succeeded in the hierarchy of printers had he returned from the war.

WARD RITCHIE

GREGG ANDERSON

GREGG AND CAROLINE ANDERSON, 1944

FROM LEFT TO RIGHT: GREGG ANDERSON (LEFT) AT THE AGE OF EIGHT WITH HIS BROTHER; A FRESHMAN AT POMONA COLLEGE READY FOR FOOTBALL PRACTICE; DURING HIS COLLEGE YEARS.

WITH HIS AUNT, SUMMER OF 1929.

THE SPRING OF 1944 IN ENGLAND, SHORTLY BEFORE D-DAY.

TWO VIEWS OF THE GRABHORN PRESS IN 1931, AT THE TIME GREGG ANDERSON WAS WORKING THERE AS COMPOSITOR.

GREGG ANDERSON, THIRD FROM LEFT, AT A MERIDEN GRAVURE COMPANY PICNIC IN BARKHAMSTED, CONNECTICUT ON JULY 12, 1934.

GREGG ANDERSON, LEFT FOREGROUND, INTENT ON A GAME AT THE SAME PICNIC AS IN THE TOP PICTURE.

THE PRESSROOM NOOK OF THE WARD RITCHIE PRESS IN 1935 WHEN IT WAS LOCATED IN AN OLD RANCH HOUSE.

ANOTHER VIEW OF THE GRIFFITH PARK BOULEVARD SHOP OF THE WARD RITCHIE PRESS SHOWING THE COMPOSING ROOM.

THE OFFICE OF ANDERSON & RITCHIE ON HYPERION AVENUE IN 1940.

A PARTIAL VIEW OF THE PRESSROOM OF ANDERSON & RITCHIE IN 1940.

BIBLIOGRAPHY OF

Gregg Anderson

1926-1942

Compiled by
LAWRENCE CLARK POWELL

Foreword

My contribution to this bibliography has been to compile the data furnished by Gregg's partners, Roland Baughman and Ward Ritchie. This is not a full-dress bibliographical description of the Anderson imprints; it is rather a simple check-list which establishes what Gregg printed and when.

My friendship with Gregg was slow in getting started. I met him first in 1929 when Ward and I were sharing a studio at Clyde Browne's Abbey San Encino, but it was not until he returned to Los Angeles in 1936 that we began to get acquainted. About the time I went to work at UCLA in 1938 I appointed myself Librarian and Bibliographer of the Ward Ritchie Press, and from that time until his death six years later Gregg and I became increasingly good friends.

A number of common interests drew us together: printing done for me by the Press, including a bookplate by Gregg, a memorial to my brother, a 70th birthday book for my mother, the collecting and cataloging of Anderson and Ritchie imprints, the Rounce and Coffin Club, and so forth. It was sheer delight to work with Gregg. He was practical and punctual and he shared my librarian's passion for accuracy. Nothing upset him. He had great patience and tact, and an unfailing, puckish sense of humor.

After he entered the service we exchanged occasional letters. I heard from him a last time in a letter from England, two weeks before the invasion; about two months later Ward phoned me the news of Gregg's death in Normandy. I cannot express the sense of personal loss I felt and still feel, but the loss to printing was far greater. If anyone could have grown into Updike's shoes it was Gregg Anderson.

L.C.P.

EARLY PRINTING, INCLUDING IMPRINTS OF THE GREY BOW PRESS

The collations and notes in this section are entirely the work of Roland Baughman, Gregg's partner in the Grey Bow Press. Reference should be made also to the Grey Bow Press check-list contributed by Gregg to Will Ransome's *Private Presses and Their Books* (1929). The only complete collection of these items is in the Huntington Library, established by Roland Baughman, Robert Schad and Mrs. Gregg Anderson.

George Gissing, a collection of essays [by Cornelius Weygandt, Paul Elmer More, and John W. Cunliffe]

Pasadena: Gregg S. Anderson, MDCCCCXXVI 75 pages [August, 1926]

Six copies only were printed, each numbered at the press. Gregg included this title in the list of Grey Bow Press imprints which he sent to Will Ransome in 1929, but the Press was not started until the following year.

Full Fathom Five, by Will Shakespeare.

[Pasadena: Gregg Anderson, 1927] Leaflet [April, 1927]

Directly responsible for the birth of the Grey Bow Press. Gregg brought it to work with him one Monday morning, and during the discussion that followed we laid the basic plan for the Press. The leaflet is interesting for its attempt to show the title words in progressively deeper shades of blue, accomplished by hand inking.

Song by Arthur O'Shaughnessy [from *Music and Moonlight*]

[Pasadena] Grey Bow [1927] 4 leaves [July, 1927]

The first item to bear the Gray Bow imprint. The text, in black, is within red rule borders in the Nash tradition. Composition and printing were wholly Gregg's.

Epithalamium to Dorothy and Phillip, a roundel [by Roland Baughman] Fecit Rollo MCMXXVII Leaflet [July, 1927]

Printed in black, red, and blue. My setting, Gregg's printing. About ten copies were printed as a wedding gift to two of my friends.

To a poet a thousand years hence, by James Elroy Flecker.

[Pasadena: Grey Bow Press] MCMXXVII
Leaflet [August, 1927]

Gregg's setting and printing.

William Butler Yeats, The Lake Isle of Innisfree.

[Pasadena] Grey Bow Press, 1927. Leaflet [October, 1927]

Gregg's setting and printing.

Old Letters [poem, so-called, by Roland Baughman]

[Pasadena] Grey Bow [1927] Leaflet [November, 1927]

My setting, Gregg's printing.

Autumn, ballade to decrepitude [by Roland Baughman]

[Pasadena] Grey Bow Press, 1927. Leaflet [November, 1927]

My setting, Gregg's printing. I adventured unsuccessfully with the ballade form, setting the three stanzas and the envoy in a solid column of type.

One hundred and thirty quatrains by Curtius Soredd & translated by R. O. B.

Pasadena: Grey Bow Press, 1928. 44 pages [January, 1928]

The most ambitious achievement of the Press, although several of the later pieces are decidedly better specimens of typography. It had been planned from the start—I was to write it and Gregg was to print it. A prospectus and order slip were issued in April, asking for subscriptions at $2.50 per copy, and promising delivery by July 1. We ordered the paper on April 20 and began setting at once. I could not compose the text fast enough to keep pace with Gregg's setting, and when July came we had made only a fair start on the project. Accordingly a "Notice to Subscribers" was sent out, explaining the delay. More months went by. We spent week-end after week-end setting, printing, and distributing. The supply of type (Century) was limited, and we dared not tie up more of it than we could handle in a single session. The finished book is therefore a bibliographical puzzle, some sheets being in folio and others in quarto. The patience of H. J. Arnold, in whose shop we did all this, was the patience of Job. The book was released in January of 1928, some six months overdue. Seventy-five copies were printed, twenty-five being on Fabriano hand-made and the balance on Warren's Oldstyle. About half were bound by D. F. Bogardus, the Warren's copies in marbled boards and black cloth spines and the Fabriano copies in batique boards with leather spines. I doubt that Bogardus was ever paid in full for his work.

The City in the Sea, by Edgar A. Poe.

[Pasadena] Grey Bow Press, 1928. Leaflet, in wrapper. [February, 1928]

Gregg's setting and printing, representing his first venture into the Meynell school of design.

Remembered One: epilogue, by Roland Baughman.

Pasadena: Grey Bow, 1928. Leaflet, in wrapper [March, 1928]

Joint venture, but mainly Gregg's work.

Out of the Past, by Llewelyn Powys.

Pasadena: Grey Bow Press, 1928. 11 pages, printed wrapper [August, 1928]

Wholly Gregg's work. With the possible exception of "Six Poems" it is the best specimen of typography issued by the Press. Printed from A.T.F. Garamond, which Gregg had bought for himself.

Six Poems [by Roland Baughman]

Pasadena: Grey Bow Press, 1928. 10 pages, printed wrapper [August, 1928]

Partially Baughman's setting, Gregg's printing. Only twelve copies were printed, most of which have happily disappeared.

Proverbs of Hell, by William Blake.

Pasadena: Grey Bow Press, 1929. Leaflet, in wrapper [January, 1929]

Gregg's printing and setting, done during his Christmas vacation from Pomona College. The type, Lutetia, belonged to Arthur M. Ellis, who also had the intention of providing an Albion hand-press for Gregg's exclusive use. This, the last imprint to bear the Grey Bow Press certification, was prepared "for private distribution, and especially for Arthur M. Ellis."

Body's Breviary, Joseph Warren Beach.

Pasadena: 1930. 30 pages, printed wrapper [January, 1930]

Gregg completed this just before he left for San Francisco. There were two varieties, one on handmade paper for presentation to the members of the Zamorano Club, and the other on newsprint with a special colophon: "Of an edition privately pirated by Gregg Anderson this is copy number—." It was not strictly piracy—at worst it was venial piracy—for Gregg tried to obtain the author's permission. As it happened, Beach couldn't be reached, being on leave from the University of Minnesota. When he returned from abroad he forgave Gregg, as attested in his letter laid in the Huntington Library copy. The printing was done during Christmas vacation at the press in the Abbey San Encino at Garvanza.

The Song of Honour, by Ralph Hodgson.

San Francisco: 1930. 14 leaves, bound. [December, 1930]

A gift book, produced by Gregg for presentation at the Christmas season of 1930-31. The colophon reads: "75 copies of this edition printed by Gregg Anderson with wood cuts by LeRoy Proctor." In a letter of January, 1931, to Wilbur Macey Stone, Gregg wrote that Hazel Dreis was to bind the lot, which was to be split three ways, but that he had received only ten copies for himself. Miss Dreis recently stated that she thinks many copies may still be among her effects, unbound.

UNFINISHED BOOKS

A Song, by Robert Bridges, the Poet Laureate of England.

Printed at the Grey Bow Press in Pasadena for distribution to friends, MCMXXVIII. Leaflet. [Summer? 1928]

The set of proof-sheets now in the Huntington Library is the only evidence that this project was ever undertaken. The poem is the well-known one beginning "I love all beauteous things . . ."

Snatches from Jeremy Taylor. [1929]

This project was apparently undertaken for Arthur M. Ellis during the summer of 1929. It was never completed. There is a proof strike of the first section in the Huntington Library.

Depression & the Anderson-McDonald Plan, an open letter to printers who sit up nights worrying about business. By two apprentices also worried. [1931?]

Only proof-sheets of the first pages are known to exist. Gregg and Thomas McDonald joined the staff of the Grabhorn Press during 1930. Apparently this was the product of some of their after-hours effort. Proofs in the Huntington Library.

MINOR PIECES

Exercise Title-Pages

By the Ionian Sea, written by George Gissing.
[Pasadena] Gregg Anderson, MDCCCCVI [sic] [Autumn? 1926]

March Winds, by A. E. Coppard.

[Pasadena, California] Gregg Anderson, 1927. [January? 1927]

For many years Coppard was one of Gregg's favorite authors, and he tried to obtain the author's permission to reprint one of the shorter sketches. This title-page exists in several variants, all of the same setting, but with differing color arrangements.

The Last Word, by Jules Barbey D'Aurevilly. Translated from the French by R. O. Baughman, B.A.

Pasadena, California: Gregg Anderson, 1927. [March, 1927]

Baughman swears he never translated this. He admits to having been a bachelor at the time, but not of arts, by choice, or in the eyes of heaven.

Witter Bynner, author of Cake, an Indulgence.
Pasadena: Grey Bow Press, 1927. [August 14, 1927]

The author's name is in silver, to represent icing on a cake.

The Mystery, a poem by Ralph Hodgson.
Pasadena: Grey Bow Press, MCMXXVII. [August 14, 1927]

One copy of this contains the certificate: "Huntington Students Project No. 1. Composition by G.A. Presswork by G.A. Approved for printing by G.A. Paper: Fabriano. Type: Cloister series and Caslon Open-face. All finally finished on August 14, 1927."

Title-Pages for Special Occasions

A History of the American Bartender, by Ralph Jenner Gifford, Haig Professor of Social Customs in DeWar University. In Vino Veritas.

Cosmopolis: Printed for the Subscribers, 1927. [August, 1927]

Copy prepared by Robert Schad; set and printed by Gregg. One copy was bound by D. F. Bogardus for presentation to Ralph Gifford on his birthday, August 16. It had many blank leaves, between which were inserted various liquor labels—rare then, unobtainable now.

Some Account of the Welcome given to Robert O. Schad on his return to Civilization after travels. Pasadena: Grey Bow Press, 1927. [September, 1927]

Schad had driven to Vancouver for his vacation; this awaited him on his return. Set and printed by Gregg.

Greeting Cards

Harry J. Arnold, Printer. Happy Birthday. [November, 1926?]

Birthday greeting from Gregg to Arnold. Only one copy has survived.

Merry Christmas, Happy New Year, 1926 & '27. Robert O. Schad. [December, 1926]

This was the first serious commission undertaken by Gregg of which there remains any record.

Roland O. Baughman [1901-1927]. Hoping that your twenty-sixth year may be as well done as your twenty-fifth, but doubting it somewhat seriously. [November, 1927]

Birthday greeting from Gregg to Baughman. He had to guess at the date of birth, and got it a year early.

To Phil ... from Rollo ... at Christmas-time, 1927 [December, 1927]

Christmas greeting from Baughman to Phillip J. Rulon. Baughman's setting, Gregg's printing.

Announcements

Prospectus of "Quatrains of Curtius" with order form. [April, 1927]

Announcement of delay in publication of "Quatrains." [July 15, 1927]

Announcement of opening of R. V. Sowers' "Burlington Art Shop" in Pasadena, October 28. [October, 1927?]

This was one of the few business commissions accepted by Gregg during this period.

Announcement of a sale of books, etc., by Gregg and his room-mate, John Cage, while they were students at Pomona College. [October? 1929]

Gregg mentioned this item in a letter to Wilbur Macey Stone, October 21, 1929. It was apparently a recent printing at that time.

Bookplates

Anderson, Gregg [1926]

"Gregg Anderson His Book" (within border formed by alphabet).

Anderson, Gregg [1926]

"Ex Libris 26 Gregg Anderson"

Baughman, Roland [1927]

"Ex Pluteo Roland O. Baughman"

Baughman, Roland

"From Roland Baughman Greetings and this book." (Gift label)

Baughman, Roland [1929]

"Nina & Roly Baughman have a book."

Sykes, Ethel [1928?]

"The Book of Ethel Sykes"

Forms

Bill Head [1926]

"Gregg Anderson, Printer." The demarcation for the entry of items is formed by the words: "Aldus Morris Gutenberg Bodoni Rogers Caslon Walker Cobden-Sanderson: These were truly printers."

Letterhead and envelope [1927]

Letterhead: "from Robert O. Schad, Pasadena, California." Envelope: "Robert O. Schad. Box Sixty-four, Pasadena, California."

Letterhead [1927]

"Henry E. Huntington Library, San Gabriel, California. Office of the Curator."

Bill Head [1928]

"Grey Bow Press, Pasadena, California," etc.

GREY BOW PRESS REDIVIVUS (1936-1939)

The Book Club of California, a selection of some of its publications dealing with California life and letters, exhibited at the Huntington Library, July-September, 1937.
[Los Angeles: Grey Bow Press, 1937]
Broadside [July, 1937]
A fairly small edition was printed for the Library, but the Book Club authorized a reprint of 500 copies for its own use.

The Vision of Joel Barlow, by Leon Howard. Los Angeles: The Grey Bow Press, 1937. 31 pages, printed wrappers [August 26, 1937]

The revived Grey Bow Press was interested primarily in the publication not of reprints, but of original works. This essay has never been published in any other form. Its author was then Assistant Professor of English at Pomona College. Twenty-five copies were especially certified as Keepsake 24 of the Columbiad Club.

Mad Blake, a poem by Will Rose Benet. Los Angeles: [Grey Bow Press] 1937. Leaflet, in wrapper. [Autumn, 1937]

Composed and printed entirely by E. G. Davies, who does not deny that Gregg's voice prompted him and Gregg's hand guided him. The Press name occurs in the colophon.

Rounce & Coffin Club Honorable Discharge. [Los Angeles: Grey Bow Press, 1938] Broadside [July 20, 1938]

Printed from pied type in purple and green ink on a proof press, for presentation to Grant Dahlstrom, in recognition of the selection of his *The Kachinas are Coming* as one of the Fifty Books, 1937.

Soaring Aloof: or, Neddy Warren's Adventure. The stories of the first American balloon ascension, by Theodore Hornberger. [1938-39]

This essay was written especially for the Grey Bow Press by Theodore Hornberger, then Research Fellow at the Huntington Library. Dr. Hornberger was himself a member of the Press. The project was never completed, and only the copy, some proofs of the early pages, and a few trial title-pages now remain.

THE TIMOTHY PRESS
MERIDEN, CONNECTICUT

The following items are known for sure to have been printed by Gregg Anderson while he was employed by the Meriden Gravure Company of Meriden, Connecticut, from 1932 to 1935. His friend and associate was E. Harold Hugo, of the Meriden Company, who stimulated and collaborated with Gregg during this period, much as did Baughman and Ritchie in earlier and later years

Services for Ella Shepardson Young Goss. 1933

The Folger Shakespeare Library, Washington. Published for the Trustees of Amherst College. 1933.

Letters and Poems from Abroad. By Nellie Hurlbut Whitney.

Some Notes on Early Connecticut Printing. By Albert Carlos Bates. Reprinted from the Papers of the Bibliographical Society of America. Meriden, Connecticut, 1934.

Recollections of the Grabhorn Press. By Gregg Anderson. Privately printed, Meriden, Connecticut, 1935.

Colophon: 70 copies printed by Gregg Anderson and Harold Hugo, of which 30 are for sale. Frontispiece in collotype by The Meriden Gravure Company. Decoration by Valenti Angelo.
The 30 copies for sale bear title-page imprint: Los Angeles, The Primavera Press, 1935.

The De Vinne and Marion Presses. A chapter from the Autobiography of Frank E. Hopkins. Meriden, the Columbiad Club, 1936.

315 copies printed at the Timothy Press.

1919 in Nineteen Thirty-five. Published for the Class of 1919, Yale College.
5¾ x 9; pp.vi, 113; blue paper cover.
New Haven, Connecticut, 1935.

Shakespeare's Titus Andronicus. The First Quarto, 1594. Reproduced in facsimile from the unique copy in the Folger Shakespeare Library with an introduction by Joseph Quincy Adams.
5¾ x 7¾; pp.41, 76 pages as of original; red cloth. Connecticut, 1936

ANDERSON & RITCHIE

Although their partnership was not formed until 1936, Gregg and Ward collaborated on several items four years earlier before Gregg went to Meriden. In addition to the following books Gregg designed a host of commercial ephemera during the six active years of the partnership. Many such pieces, as well as all of the Anderson-Ritchie books, are contained in the collection of their work which I formed and which in 1946 I gave to the William Andrews Clark Memorial Library at the University of California in Los Angeles.

In Galilee. By Hildegarde Flanner. 1932.
A Christmas piece. Title-page by Ritchie, text by Anderson.

Libros Californianos, Or Five Feet of California Books. By Phil Townsend Hanna. Los Angeles, Jake Zeitlin: Primavera Press, 1932.

American Letter, for Gerald Murphy. By Archibald MacLeish. Arroyo Grande, 1935.

The Letters of Western Authors. Number 12, December 1935. Jack London. With Comment by Charmian Kittredge London. Published for its members by The Book Club of California.

The Origin of the Species. By Charles Darwin. (Quarter Books No. 1, 1935)
No more published.

Daily Meditations. By Philip Pain. Reproduced from the original edition of 1668 in the Huntington Library. With an Introduction by Leon Howard. San Marino, Henry E. Huntington Library and Art Gallery, 1936.

Fine Books. An Exhibition of Written and Printed Books Selected for Excellence of Design, Craftsmanship and Materials. San Marino, California, Henry E. Huntington Library and Art Gallery, 1936.

An Itinerant House. By Emma Frances Dawson. With a Foreword by Paul Jordan-Smith. (The California Literary Pamphlets Number Four.) Published for its members by The Book Club of California, August, 1936.

Wheel of Fire, By Hugo Seelig. With a Foreword by Ella Young. Oceano, Round Table Book Co., 1936.

The Gay Thomas Cook Book. By Gertrude Thomas. Illustrations by Campbell Grant. Omaha, Nebraska, Mrs. Amos Thomas, 1937.

Practical Guides to Integrative Education Series No. 1. The Study of Children, Their Environment and Activities in the School as a Democratic Society. By Ethel I Salisbury, Associate Professor of Elementary Education, University of California at Los Angeles. 1937.

Practical Guides to Integrative Education Series No. 3. Reading in the Integrative Education Program. By Ethel I. Salisbury. 1937.

Sporting Books in the Huntington Library. Compiled by Lyle H. Wright. San Marino, California, 1937.

California Institute Associates. 1938.

An Exhibition of William Blake's Water-color Drawings of Milton's "Paradise Lost." May 12-July 31, 1936. San Marino, Henry E. Huntington Library and Art Gallery, 1938.

The Grabhorn Press. A Catalogue of Imprints in the Collection of Henry R. Wagner. Los Angeles, The Ward Ritchie Press, 1938.
Also another issue with following imprint: Los Angeles, California, Privately Printed, 1938.

Shakespeare's Hamlet. The Second Quarto, 1604. Reproduced in facsimile from the copy in the Huntington Library. With an Introduction by Oscar James Campbell. San Marino, 1938.

American Fiction, 1774-1850. A Contribution toward a Bibliography. By Lyle H. Wright. San Marino, California, 1939.

The Thacher School Semicentennial Addresses. Addresses Delivered . . . Commemorating The Fiftieth Anniversary of the Founding of the Thacher School by Sherman D. Thacher. Ojai, California, 1939.

Willard Samuel Morse, a Great Collector. By Henry R. Wagner. Printed for Dawson's Book Shop by The Ward Ritchie Press, November, 1939.

German Dramatists! of the 19th Century. By F. W. Kaufman of Oberlin College. Lymanhouse, Los Angeles, California. 1940.

Great Books in Great Editions. An Exhibition Commemorating the 500th Anniversary of the Invention of Printing. The Huntington Library, San Marino, California. 1940.

The American Journal of Ambrose Serle, Secretary to Lord Howe 1776-1778. Edited with an Introduction by Edward G. Tatum jr. The Huntington Library, San Marino, California. 1940.

American Manuscript Collections in the Huntington Library, for the History of the Seventeenth and Eighteenth Centuries. Compiled by Norma B. Cuthbert. San Marino, California, The Huntington Library, 1941.

Collecting, Especially Books. By Henry R. Wagner. Los Angeles, 1941.
30 copies for the author.
30 copies for the Columbiad Club.
30 copies for the Rounce and Coffin Club.

Life and Its Problems, As Viewed by a Blind Man at the Age of Ninety-six. By Joseph Widney. Edited by T. Cameron Taylor. Hollywood, California, Joseph P. Widney Publications, 1941.

Bullion to Books. Fifty Years of Business and Pleasure. By Henry R. Wagner. Los Angeles, The Zamorano Club, 1942.

The California Almanac for 1849. By Benjamin Greenleaf. Reprinted from the copy in the Huntington Library. San Marino, California, Friends of the Huntington Library, 1942.

A Discourse upon the Exposicion & Understanding of Statutes. With Sir Thomas Egerton's Additions. Edited from Manuscripts in the Huntington Library. By Samuel E. Thorne. San Marino, California, The Huntington Library, 1942.

Glances at California, 1847-1853. Diaries and Letters of William Rich Hutton, Surveyor. With a Brief Memoir and Notes by Willard O. Waters. San Marino, The Huntington Library, 1942.
Title-page by Ritchie, rest of book by Anderson.

The Work of the Merrymount Press and Its Founder Daniel Berkeley Updike (1860-1941). An Exhibition Prepared by Gregg Anderson. San Marino, California, The Huntington Library, 1942.

Poems of Hua Lo. By Lowell C. Frost. Los Angeles, California. 1942.

Printed at the Cole-Holmquist Press